The Best Kept SECRETS in the KINGDOM

20 KEYS GUARANTEED TO REVOLUTIONIZE YOUR LIFE & YOUR CHURCH

Andy R. Taylor

The Best Kept **SECRETS** in the KINGDOM

Copyright © 2020 Andy R Taylor
ISBN: 9798645673734
Library of Congress Control Number: 2020912498
Published in the United States of America

All rights reserved as permitted under the U. S. Copyright Act of 1976. No part of this publication may be reproduced, distributed, or transmitted in any form or by any means, or stored in a database or retrieval system, without the expressed written permission of the author and publisher.

Unless otherwise noted, all Scripture quotations are taken from the *New King James* Version®. Copyright © 1982 by Thomas Nelson, Inc. Used by permission. All rights reserved.

Scriptures mark Amplified Bible are taken from *The Amplified Bible*, copyright ©2015 by The Lockman Foundation, La Habra, CA 90631. All rights reserved.

www.BurkhartBooks.com
Bedford, Texas

Dedication

To Julie

My Wife for going on 44 years, the best Mom our six kids could've ever hoped for, and a Hall of Fame MeMe to our ten grandkids (so far!). You're the wind to my sail, my reason for staying the course, and a constant inspiration to always give it my best. Who could've dreamed that two kids on a movie date at age 13 could possibly still be together 53 years later, and with an incredible Tribe now numbering 20! There have been plenty of ups and downs—all the normal challenges and a few disappointments—along the way, but with the help of the Lord and undying love for one another, here we are! As good as our life has been, I still believe the best years are in front of us. You're everything I need.

I love you so much.

Acknowledgments

The Family of Trinity Fellowship

This truly genuine Family of Kingdom people has served as the laboratory for these principles to be fleshed out. Thanks for your faithfulness, your support, and encouragement, as well as your determination to "stay the course!"

Buddy Suthers and Eric Easter

Your wisdom, insight, and stark honesty on some of the harder chapters have been more valuable than you could ever know. Thanks!

Ben Fike

Father, Mentor, Confidant, and Friend. Thanks for your diligence to help make *The Best Kept Secrets In The Kingdom* a better book! I'm eternally grateful.

Johnny Buckner and Rope Myers

Thanks for the suggestions, encouragement, and constructive criticism. Early on, your words caused *The Best Kept Secrets In The Kingdom* to go from just an idea to a reality!

Tim Taylor - Burkhart Books

Thanks, Tim, for your always steady and wise counsel. Oh, and your patience, too!

My kids and Their Families:

A truly incredible group that is always an inspiration for me to do better!

- Clint & Kristy, Cooper, Dailee, Preslie, and Crockett
- Cade, Allie
- Cole & Kelly, Calli, Maverick, and Knox
- Clay & Chelsea, Timber, and Asa Cliff
- Cord, who is waiting for us in Heaven
- Cameron

Contents

Dedication	
Acknowledgments	
Foreword	11
Introduction	13
The Life Saving Station	15
Simplicity	17
The Church, What Is It?	21
The Kingdom of God	33
One Church	43
Building With Vision	49
Building on Relationships	59
Equipping the Saints	67
Contending For Signs And Wonders	73
Spiritual Gifts	81
Moving in the Prophetic	91
Church Government	103
Toward More Powerful Prayer	117
The Pursuit of True Worship	127
What Is the Lord Saying?	137
Ministry to The Poor	143
Understanding Grace	149
Developing a Healthy Giving Culture	159
Embracing Destiny	167
Shaping An Agape Culture	171
Displacing the Religious Spirit	175
Conclusion: If The Church is Going to be The Church	181
Who is God?	185
Trinity Fellowship Vision	187
About the Author	

Foreword

As I write these words, the world is in the midst of transition like never before; moments that will go down in history are unfolding right in front of us. Unrest has gripped the hearts of many, and fatigue has begun to set in. Still, if there was ever a time made for Believers to arise and shine, it's now. The truth is, as cultural architects, as apostolic leaders and ministers of reconciliation, the posture of our hearts is—we get to do this!

As a source of personal strength, I meditate on the scene recorded in Luke 4:16-20. You may recall this passage—the moment when Jesus entered the synagogue on a Sabbath morning, turned to the magistrate, and was handed the scroll of Isaiah. Arriving at the 61st chapter, Jesus read aloud what was known as the Messiah's Mandate. The room grew still and intensely quiet; every eye focused their attention on Jesus as He made his way over to what history records as the Messiah's Chair—a chair placed in the front of the synagogue which remained empty for hundreds of years as it had been reserved for their promised King. Jesus took His seat.

I find great solace in knowing that Jesus has not only taken His rightful place on the throne, but He still reigns! Yet, the verses in Isaiah 61 remind me that there is work still to do, and I believe it's one of the reasons why Andy Taylor has loyally labored to put this book, *The Best Kept Secrets In The Kingdom*, in your hands.

Throughout these pages, Andy does what he does best—he builds leaders. The legacy of his life gives weight to the words he so carefully composed in this book for those called to disciple, lead, and equip. In a way that only an apostolic leader can, *The Best Kept Secrets In The Kingdom*, revives that sacred moment when those first called by God took hold of the biblical mandate to disciple the nations.

This book is a timely response, as God is moving mightily amid earth's complex challenges right now and asking His Church to engage the world proactively. *The Best Kept Secrets In The Kingdom* is a divine set up! As you pour over the pages of this book, you'll see a Kingdom blueprint with detailed action steps and insightful resources that will bring about transformation in not only your life but also your home, your city, and your nation!

Kris Vallotton
Bethel Church,
Redding, CA

Introduction

"It is customary to blame secular science and anti-religious philosophy for the eclipse of religion in modern society. It would be more honest to blame religion for its own defeats. Religion declined not because it was refuted, but because it became irrelevant, dull, oppressive, insipid. When faith is completely replaced by creed, worship by discipline, love by habit; when the crisis of today is ignored because of the splendor of the past; when faith becomes an heirloom rather than a living fountain; when religion speaks only in the name of authority rather than with the voice of compassion—its message becomes meaningless."
—Abraham Joshua Heschel (*God in Search of Man*, 1955)

Heschel was onto something 65 years ago when he penned this paragraph. I'm afraid his comments have become distressingly prophetic. In many cases, the situation has just gotten worse. The church and its message of Jesus and His Kingdom is the hope of the world. In many cases, the church has lost sight of its prophetic destiny. As a result, many of her people have also grown apathetic and disinterested. A number of years back the Lord quietly said to my spirit:

"Andy, the one organism on the planet I have designed to give the world hope is destroying their hope."

This book was born at least 20 years ago in my heart. As a leader, I began to notice very important issues that, in my opinion, had somehow lost their value and importance to the masses in our generation. I have no intention to be critical, much less condemning of the state of the modern church. I pray that comes through loud and clear throughout the pages of this book. In fact, I'm talking to myself as much as anyone. My deep love for the Body of Christ and a nagging sense of dissatisfaction of where I see the church today (my own included!) in terms of the absence of supernatural power and genuine agape love leaves me with a strong resolve to do whatever I can to bring profound change for the better in the Body. The church, even in its current state and with all its flaws and imperfections considered, is still the only organism the Father has given the authority and power to bring revival, renewal, transformation and Kingdom revolution to the earth.

The principles listed in this book have come from 30 years of experience and observation. *The Best Kept Secrets In The Kingdom* serves as an easy to understand overview of subjects that either have been overlooked, ignored, or have simply been forgotten in the church's list of priorities. If you're looking for an exhaustive study on the topics I have written about here you will be sorely disappointed. That hasn't been my intention at all. In fact, for every chapter I have written, there have been volumes of books written about the very same subjects. The challenge in writing *The Best Kept Secrets In The Kingdom* is giving enough information on the subjects to spark an interest that will, hopefully, cause the reader to want to dig deeper, do more research, get the needed help from the Holy Spirit, and to come away with deeper convictions that lead to decisive action.

This book is for every person sitting in church on any given Sunday quietly wondering if by chance there could be more to church life than what they have experienced to date. It's for anyone in the Body of Christ, young or old, new convert or seasoned veteran who longs to see the Body of Christ transformed into its purest and most powerful form. This book is like any instructional book in that you might be presented with new information, new ideas or a fresh perspective but nothing really happens unless, or until, one puts the principles to the test. J.C. Penney was right when he said, "Theory is splendid, but until put into practice, it is valueless." The principles put forth in this book will help you to blossom and flourish as a child of God. They will equip even others to be successful leaders in the Body of Christ with the ability to lead their flock beyond the normal conservative, denominational and religious constraints. But what's even more important than that, we'll have the opportunity to experience authentic Christianity—how it really should be! We get to be a part of helping the Father show it to the rest of the world!

I believe we're supposed to be better than we currently are. I'm convinced the glory of God to come is greater than anything the world has ever experienced. While it will take commitment and hard work, the solution is simple. The church has an appointment with destiny. You are here for that reason! The clock is ticking. We have lots to look forward to, but no time to waste.

Andy Taylor

THE LITTLE LIFE SAVING STATION
Anthony de Mello (1931-1987)

"On a rocky seacoast where shipwrecks were frequent there was once a ramshackle little lifesaving station. It was no more than a hut and there was only one boat, but the few people who manned the station were a devoted lot who kept constant watch over the sea with little regard for themselves and their safety, went fearlessly out in a storm if they had any evidence that there had been a shipwreck somewhere. Many lives were thus saved and the station became famous.

As the fame of the station grew, so did the desire of people in the neighborhood to become associated with its excellent work. They generously offered of their time and money, so new members were enrolled, new boats bought, and new crews trained. The hut, too, was replaced by a comfortable building which could adequately handle the needs of those who had been saved from the sea and, of course, since shipwrecks do not occur everyday, it became a popular gathering place … a sort of local club.

As time passed the members became so engaged in socializing that they had little interest in lifesaving, though they duly sported the lifesaving motto on the badges they wore. As a matter of fact, when some people were actually rescued from the sea, it was always such a nuisance because they were dirty and sick and soiled the carpeting and the furniture.

Soon the social activities of the club became so numerous and the lifesaving activities so few that there was a showdown at a club meeting, with some members insisting that they return to their original purpose and activity. A vote was taken and these troublemakers, who proved to be a small minority, were invited to leave the club and start another.

Which is precisely what they did … a little further down the coast, with such selflessness and daring that, after a while, their heroism made them famous. Whereupon their membership was enlarged, their hut was reconstructed … and their idealism smothered. If you happen to visit the area today, you will find a number of exclusive clubs dotting the shoreline. Each one of them is justifiably proud of its origin and its tradition. Shipwrecks still occur in those parts, but nobody seems to care much."

Simplicity

"Simplicity is the ultimate sophistication"
—Leonardo Da Vinci

Even though many would argue, Leonardo had a very valid point! There's something extremely intriguing about simplicity. Simplicity evens the playing field for everyone and has the innate ability to bring anyone/everyone to a better place no matter what the issues in question might be. We live in a religious environment that nearly always ignores simple precepts, ideas and solutions in favor of things more complicated. Simplicity escalates and gives momentum to the establishment of the Kingdom of God in the earth! That's why simplicity should always be included in *The Best Kept Secrets In The Kingdom*.

It appears Paul saw a potentially approaching danger of believers moving away from the simplicity of Jesus and the good news when he said, "But I fear, lest somehow, as the serpent deceived Eve by his craftiness, so your minds may be corrupted from the simplicity that is in Christ." 2 Corinthians 11:3 Paul's ministry to the Gentiles caused him to be challenged on a regular basis by the Jewish lawyers (interpreters of the Old Testament Law), the Scribes, and Pharisees. They routinely treated him with scorn, ridicule and contempt. But where knowledge was concerned, no group was more challenging than the Greek philosophers. Their approach to wisdom and knowledge deemed the gospel of Jesus Christ to be way too simple. For the most part, they rejected Paul and his message. They had a strong following and were very persuasive in speech as to sway new converts away from the simplicity that's in Christ. We should be cautious in our own pursuit of truth that we don't allow our minds to be manipulated away from the simplicity of the good news.

Twenty years ago I found myself in the presence of half a dozen guys I would classify as, world changers. I've since become great friends with all these men. They're guys I would call "big brothers" in the Lord. Each of them displayed a strong anointing in their lives ranging from being great leaders, great authors, trusted prophets, awesome teachers, great communicators, etc. I could easily see how valuable they were to the Lord and His plan on the earth. I learned so much from these men, but I wondered how I got into the picture. I couldn't see how I could add anything of value to the equation, and I was totally blind to anything I could actually offer them.

I asked the Lord, "How did I get here?" "What could I possibly add to this group they don't already have?" Almost as quickly as I asked, I heard the Lord say, "Andy, you bring simplicity to the table." Right on the heels of that, He said, "I'm about to bring the prominence to simplicity it has always deserved."

That opened a door of understanding and awareness of how the Lord has blessed me and how He could use me to be effective in the Body of Christ. It was obviously an awakening, of sorts. The ability to take complex issues, simplify them to a point where anyone can understand them and then be able to clearly communicate them has now become a normal way of serving the Body, for me, over the years. I'm totally OK with not having to be the obvious intellectual in every conversation. In fact, I can now celebrate the fact that no matter how complicated a subject might be, my God-given perspective and ability enables me to bring people into a clearer understanding. If we can understand better, we're more likely to activate our faith to be a functional contributor in the Body of Christ. By the way, simplicity doesn't mean dumb, backwards, slow, or anything like that, as some might think. One of the greatest Christian authors of all time, E. Stanley Jones said it this way; "All great discoveries are a reduction of complexities to simplicity." If you think about it, Jesus had this exact same quality. He was the Son of God. He had all power and all knowledge. When He taught, it was so easily understood—even for those who had absolutely no religious or spiritual orientation, that virtually no one could miss the truth He communicated. In that way, simplicity is extremely profound!

That's my goal! Through the pages of this book, I hope you can see and appreciate the simplicity by which I've attempted to explain *The Best Kept Secrets In The Kingdom*. If I have succeeded, and if you are able to understand things that once seemed too lofty or complicated for you and are willing to add your faith to them, your life will be transformed in so many ways you'll be incredibly amazed.

PLAN OF ACTION:

- Learn to look for the simple truths in Scripture
- In your pursuit of truth always consider the simplicity of Jesus
- Keep it simple

LEADERS:

- Learn to make complex truths simple for your people
- Teach in such a way that hearers cannot miss the truth
- Keep an eye out for those that would sway your people away from the simplicity of the gospel
- Be on guard for New Age, astrology and philosophical influences that have the ability to confuse your people

PRAY:

Father, help me to see the simplicity in all that You have created. Help me to understand those things I need to know to be a mover and shaker in Your Kingdom.

The Church, What Is It?

"I will build My church and the gates of hell will not prevail against it."
—Jesus

The question seems simple enough. The Church; Just the mention of the word conjures up a myriad of thoughts and images. Some of those images would obviously have some validity—others obviously not—but what is the church? Everyone has an opinion, but what does the Bible say? The church is mentioned over seventy times in the New Testament (none in the Old). When you ask someone, "Where's the church?" their immediate answer indicates their obvious perception that it's a building or structure. The answer is nearly always to give a geographical location or the description of a building, but the Bible, in speaking of the church, never refers to a geographic location or a building, not even once. It makes one wonder then, what is the church?

The Greek word used in the Bible for church is *ekklesia*. It means "those that are called out." So, the first principle in understanding what the church actually is requires us to come to the obvious conclusion that it's a "people." The Bible refers to this group of "called out" ones in at least one instance as "peculiar." Peculiar in the sense that they look, think, behave and love in a different way than the world around them. Peculiar in the sense that they stand out from the crowd, not in an exclusive way in which nobody fits in. They are peculiar in a way that makes the world be drawn into their midst because of the love that they have, one for another. Sometimes the word, peculiar, takes on the idea of being strange, or even weird. When you think about it from a strictly humanistic standpoint I totally agree. These followers of Jesus are both strange and weird at the same time. I'm glad the world notices that they're different. In fact, when the world notices no difference at all something's seriously wrong! Being strange from the world's perspective doesn't necessarily mean off-base or wrong. In the case of the church operating as it should, it's solid evidence that something's right!

The question, "what is the church", is an important one for sure. It's tragic that many leaders in the church today really have no clear idea of what they're trying to build because they have a skewed idea of what the church is supposed to be in the first place. Most are building according to religious tradition based on what they've seen and experienced in their denominational environment. In this strategic season, we must have a resolve to build only that which the Lord desires. To do that may require forgetting some of the things we think we know about what the church should be in lieu of something profoundly different. Not just different for the sake of being different but different in ways that will cause the church to be much more effective and relevant for the times, an organism that is well equipped to change the world!

Oftentimes it makes sense to understand what something is "not," so you can best understand what it actually is. In talking about the church, if you're going to be a leader or builder, it's as important to know what "not" to build, as it is in knowing what to build! Let's examine a few of the things the church is not:

Not a Religious Entity:

Contrary to popular opinion, Jesus didn't come to start a new religion, far from it! What He did come to do was/is to establish His kingdom and to bring us into relationship with the Father. Most people would consider Christianity a religion to be listed with the hundreds of others. But Christianity is not a religion. In the first century the name, "Christians," was not an endearing term. It was the name given to those professing to be followers of Jesus and was given as a way of criticizing or making light of them. Jesus didn't come to start a religion; He came to start a relationship! So, in the strictest sense of the term, it's not a religious entity.

Not a Building:

While in modern times, even though the church does meet in buildings, the building does not make the church. You can have the nicest building around, and there's not a thing wrong with that, but take the people out and all you have is an empty building. It's interesting to note that the first designated church building didn't come along until, roughly, three hundred years after the church in the book of Acts! Up until that time, believers found it sufficient and extremely beneficial to meet in homes. One must wonder how much has actually been gained in what appears to be progress in the evolution of the church.

Not an Organization:

A church may have many of the identifying characteristics of an organization. It may have regular meetings to discuss business issues; It may be incorporated; It may have corporate officers like an organization; it might have by-laws and such things as borrowing resolutions and financial requirements. In this day and time, it would be dumb not to have some of those things. For purposes of accurately defining what the church "is," in the truest sense of the word, it is "not" an organization. A much clearer and truer definition would be that the church is an "organism." Organizations by their very nature do not have "life." Organisms on the other hand, again by their nature, do have life! We have been called out of darkness into His marvelous light into this organism called the church. It's alive! We're not members of an organization, but citizens of a kingdom!

Not a Business:

The church is not a business. Its reason for existence is not to make money. The church regularly receives tithes and offerings, which can often amount to thousands of dollars. It does this not to amass or stockpile great wealth but to use those tithes and offerings for the support of the ministry and the furtherance of the good news. Even though it makes sense to engage in wise business practices in the church today, to define the church as a business would be a clear mistake.

Not the Kingdom:

There are those who have made the erroneous assumption that the church and the kingdom are one and the same. Not true. The church is a very important part of the kingdom of God, and it is divinely and strategically included in His master plan. To say that the church and the kingdom are the same thing is monumentally wrong. The kingdom of God is a vast subject and one that needs to be looked at and studied intently. It is only as we grow in our understanding of the kingdom that every other thing comes into proper perspective. "Seek first the kingdom of God, and His righteousness, and all these other things will be added unto you."

The kingdom of God will be addressed more specifically later in this book. For now, it can be said that the church is the organism that God has given the power and authority to communicate, implement and facilitate all the facets and benefits of the kingdom of God to the world. To declare that the church and the kingdom are the same thing is to grossly misunderstand and minimize what the kingdom of God actually is. Let's not make that mistake! As important as the church is the kingdom of God is even more important! An accurate perception of the church is only possible when one begins to get an accurate perception of the kingdom!

Now let's examine a few things we know about what the church is:

The Bride of Christ:

Although the Bible doesn't use the exact phrase, Bride of Christ, it does refer to the church as a bride that's being prepared for the bridegroom. The church, at this very moment, is being prepared for Jesus, the bridegroom. How are we being prepared? By the very things you are encountering in your own church. Mountain and valley experiences, challenges, turmoil, relational conflict, seasons of favor and seasons of travail and dozens of other things that we are being tested in, and that serve to purify us as leaders and the organism as a whole. We're moving toward the Bride being ready to be presented to the bridegroom "holy and without blemish!" (Eph. 5:27).

The Body of Christ:

"Now you are the body of Christ, and members individually." 1 Cor. 12:27-28 According to Paul, the church is a many-membered body. Paul went to great lengths to explain these things to the Corinthians. He taught like Jesus in such stark simplicity that literally no one could miss the truth. In reality you and I are "body parts" in this mystical organism we call the church. I've dedicated my life to helping people find their place of gifting and anointing in the Body for two basic reasons.

1. To honor Jesus so the church will be the force in the world He wants it to be.
2. So individuals will find their purpose in life. A light bulb only displays its glory when it's plugged into a power source.

It's the same for us as individual body parts in the Body of Christ! We find our greatest fulfillment by stepping into the "call" of God on our life. As the Body of Christ the church is to do all the things that Jesus would do if He were here in the flesh. "As He is, so are we in the world" (1 John 4:17-18).

A Family:

God, being Who He is, could have taken on any identity that He wanted. He is a Father! That's His true identity!

> "God's not looking for a congregation, He's looking for a Family.
> If He wanted something other than a Family He would have called Himself something other than Father."
> —AT

That's a declaration I've made for years to the church both locally and trans-locally. It's true! It takes a while for people to catch the spirit of that. I often hear people referring to their "church family." When I hear that, it sounds shallow to me. I'm not making a judgment call on whether it actually is or not; it just feels that way to me. What I do know is the first century church definitely had it going on! There was nothing shallow about it! Agreed, the culture was much different then than now and how it would be fleshed out would definitely be different today. But there was something very significant about what was happening and I sincerely believe we can capture those essential elements and implement them today. There were, early on, in the book of Acts at least 8,120 believers in Jerusalem, 8,000 of which were brand new converts!. (120 in the upper room; 3,000 saved on the day of Pentecost; 5,000 more just a short time later!)

Along with that the Word records the Lord was adding to the church daily, those that should be saved! Again, it says that the number of disciples was being "multiplied" (Acts 2:42-45). "And they continued steadfastly in the apostles' doctrine and fellowship, in the breaking of bread, and in prayers. Then fear came upon every soul, and many wonders and signs were done through the apostles. Now all who believed were together, and had all things in common, and sold their possessions and goods, and divided them among all, as anyone had need." There was exponential growth taking place in a short time. Keep in mind, too, that there was no church building, no Bible, no man called the pastor, no committee helping to make decisions for the growing church. Yet, the church was doing so good that now, generations later we are still trying to figure out how to recapture those essential elements to grow the church. There are workshops, seminars and conferences totally devoted to church growth. I'm not against any of that. My point is this: God's purpose is for the church to be a Family and until we awaken to that and find out how you flesh-out this "Family" thing in our generation, the church will never be what She's supposed to be!

An Equipping Center:

"And He Himself gave some to be apostles, some prophets, some evangelists, and some pastors and teachers, for the equipping of the saints for the work of ministry, for the edifying of the body of Christ …" (Eph. 4:11-13). This principle, definitely one of *The Best Kept Secrets In The Kingdom*, is one that, if adhered to, can bring solid, genuine growth quicker (not that that's our goal!) than any other single thing I can think of. It also brings a sustainability factor that nothing else can bring. This issue definitely deserves a chapter of its own, so we'll discuss this more thoroughly later in this book but make no mistake about it; the church should be an equipping center to help its family members to find their place in the Body!

Hospital/Infirmary:

While I wouldn't use only these words to define the church, I would have to include them in the scope of what the church is. A hospital or infirmary is a place where people go to get treated for ailments. The church is a place where they not only can be treated but treated with the expectation that they are going to get well! One of the greatest compliments we hear about our church is, "It's a place were people get well!" Get well from what, you might ask? The church should be a place full of the grace, power, and love of God, where people get well from anything and everything that ails them! Everything across the spectrum, including physical, spiritual, emotional, relational, even financial issues, and more are able to be completely healed and remedied if we believe what the Bible says about the church.

An Army:

I hesitate just a little to include this one for the fact that I think some groups take it a little too far. There's no doubt about it; the church needs to be informed and somewhat savvy about spiritual warfare. It's true that we have an adversary. The devil is a crafty and seasoned deceiver. As Paul says, "We're not ignorant of his devices." As a leader, I'm going to train my people in some of the specifics of spiritual warfare, but I'm not going to give the enemy any more credit or air time than necessary. While I totally believe in the demonic realm, I certainly don't think that every bad, negative, or unpleasant thing has a demon behind it like some folks do. So, in defining what the church is, I'd reluctantly include "an army" on my list as long as it's kept in proper, healthy perspective.

Whose Church is it?

Jesus said, "I will build My church and the gates of hell will not prevail against it; I will give you the keys to the kingdom of heaven and whatever you bind on earth will be bound in the heavenlies, and whatever you loose on earth will be loosed in the heavenlies." It's His church! He's the Vine, we're the branches; without Him, we can do nothing. The church has spiritual "life" only when it's rightly connected to that Vine. Paul said, "husbands are to love their wives as Christ loved the church, and gave Himself for it." Part of the reason Jesus died was for the church to gloriously emerge in the earth. As much as we as leaders are to pour our lives into the church we're never to stake our own claim on it as "ours!" His church will work; it'll be effective. Yours will do neither! It's His church! We'd be wise to acknowledge that and expect to see the results of something He would build!

If it is His church, the manner of how we build becomes extremely important. Man's ideas of how the church should be are no comparison for His ideas and His pattern. Be advised that if you build the church "your" way God will bless it to some degree because it has His name on it. But if we're to expect the full blessing of God on what we're doing we definitely need to do it His way! If we're going to be kingdom builders let's resolve to build according to the Biblical pattern. Let's be determined not to build another thing that doesn't change the world!

The Church = Victorious

Some years back, the Spirit of the Lord said to me:

> "Andy, the one organism I have designed to give the world hope is destroying their hope."

In many cases, the church has become no more than a bland and benign social gathering. A maintenance mentality has crept in. Nothing supernatural is happening, and in some cases, not even talked about anymore. The people involved have been seduced to believe this is all there is. Sad when one considers the declining spiritual condition of our nation and the world, in light of the glorious mandate and incredible plan the Father obviously has for the church.

A lot of people believe the church will suffer, dwindle down, be void of any power, and be in a place where the Lord has to come back and miraculously rescue us. I'm not one of those people. I believe the church should be victorious! If not, why would Jesus and Paul give such specific and detailed instructions. Is it so we could just barely survive and hope for a victorious rescue at the end, or is it so the church could rise up in the midst of crooked and perverse generation, go against the grain of worldly, humanistic thinking and behavior to be the powerful force on earth the Lord has destined her to be? For me that's an easy question. I agree that a lot has to transpire in the life of the church of today for it to be victorious. Believing it is supposed to be victorious is a great start in seeing the full manifestation of the church in the Earth! Let's contend for "that" church and make whatever adjustments are required to see it happen!

In 1975, Bill Bright, founder of Campus Crusade and Loren Cunningham, founder of Youth With a Mission(YWAM), developed a God-given, world-changing strategy. Their mandate: Bring Godly change to a nation by reaching its seven spheres, or mountains, of societal influence. They concluded that in order to transform any nation with the Gospel of Jesus Christ truly, these seven facets of society must be reached:

- Religion
- Family
- Education
- Government
- Media
- Business
- Arts & Entertainment

I'm also a firm believer that the church should lead in all of the cultural areas. Why? Because we have an unfair advantage over non-believers in the world in that we have the supernatural help of the Holy Spirit.

My goal is not to persuade you to think like I think about the church but to get for yourself some God-given conviction of how the church is supposed to be. I will say that if you don't buy into the victorious church mentality somewhere along the way, the danger is for you to settle in and just be satisfied with a mediocre substitute.

To Sum It Up:

The Church - My Definition:

The church is an ever-changing, ever-evolving supernatural, called-out and victorious kingdom family of like-minded believers in Jesus, known for their love for one another, bonded together by the common-thread of agape love and the unity of the Holy Spirit, who are commissioned and empowered by the Father with the authority to propagate and spread the good news (by communicating & demonstrating signs and wonders) to the world and to carry out the perfect will of Jesus to co-labor with Him as He establishes His Kingdom in the Earth.

Knowing what the church is, and what it isn't, is definitely one of *The Best Kept Secrets In The Kingdom*. If you're going to be a builder, then first, understand what the church is. This is a non-negotiable issue. Building the church in our generation is definitely not for the faint of heart! "Many are called, but few are chosen" (few answer the call). For those brave enough to answer the call, all the resources of Heaven and Earth are at your disposal!

The Tendency = To build what you have seen or experienced with only a few variations.

> "We're not building something we've seen. We're building something we haven't seen!" Except in our mind/vision, as the Lord reveals, etc.*

> "We're not trying to build some nice little, quaint church that's bland, benign, and ineffective in nature. In cooperating with Jesus, we're building something that should incite a kingdom revolution in our generation!"
> —AT

"Uh, We Don't Have a Program"

When we started Trinity Fellowship nearly 32 years ago, the Lord was faithful to show us what He wanted us to help Him build and how He wanted us to build "it." We had no preconceived idea(s) as to what it should be or how it should look. So, we were dependent on what we believed He was saying to us. That only makes sense when you understand that our lives are to be lived by faith. One of the things, early on, that seemed to be clear is that we would be an organism (not organization) the Father would use to set people free. That freedom would include everything from freedom from sin, addiction, and faulty thinking to freedom from lifeless religious bondage as well.

Looking back through the years, it seems clear that the Lord has definitely kept His part of the promise, as He always does. One of the things that's been extremely rewarding has been the steady stream of people who have come to Sayre to find that "freedom." We've built some amazing friendships with folks from all over that we would have otherwise never had the privilege of knowing.

One particular case in point happened not too long ago when a person we didn't know called about a friend who had experienced a moral failure in his ministry. We didn't know the person who called, but we had been referred to him by someone we both knew.

When he called, he was understandably full of questions such as, "What do y'all do?", and "What's the Cost?", and "How do you do what you do?". I tried my best to answer all those questions, and finally, he asked, "Well, what kind of program do you have, anyway?" My reply must have taken him completely off guard; "Uh, we don't have a program." It's really true. There's not a program per se here, but what we do produces long term results. We're not batting a thousand, but we're doing pretty good. Here are some reasons why;

We first bring them into our 'circle'. It's not an inner circle because inner circles are, by nature, exclusive. We're inclusive!

We let them be a part of whatever it is that we're doing at the time. If we're on a ministry project, they come along, and they might even help if they're willing. We never apply pressure on them to do that, but the door's always open for them to participate. If we're going to lunch, they go. If we're going to a basketball game, they go too. We let them know that they're an important part of our family.

We let them see the 'real' side of us. We refuse to put up the facade of perfection. Truth is, we're far from it. Besides, it's just not our style!

We're learners, and we help to develop that trait in them, by seeing us do it, while they're here.

We spend quality time with them. We swap stories. We listen to their story. They listen to ours! It's a great way to build long-term relationships. And, that's what we're all about.

We help them to understand the Father's love for them. We encourage them to connect relationally with the Father, and we explain how easy that is.

We treat 'em like VIP's....... 'cause they are!

But more important than all the other stuff, we just love 'em. It never fails, you know! It's undefeated! And it always works!

The Lord always does His part.....which is just about everything!

But, program, uh, we don't have a program.

This and more thoughts from Andy can be found at his blog: "The Way I See It" - www.andyrtaylor.com.

PLAN OF ACTION:

- Continue to pursue how the Lord wants the church to look in your generation
- As your understanding grows, commit to adapt to your new mindset
- Resist the temptation to "settle in;" Keep moving
- Find your place in the Body and begin to function there

LEADERS:

- Implement change slowly and deliberately based on your growing understanding of what the church should be
- Encourage your people to embrace change
- Continue moving as the Lord moves
- Stay the course

PRAY:

Father, open my eyes to the importance of the church. Give me a healthy perception of where the church is and where You want it to go. Help me to be a part of the Body that's functioning.

RESOURCE:

- *The Church in the New Testament* by Kevin Conner

The Kingdom of God

"Seek first the Kingdom of God and His righteousness,
and all these other things will be added unto you."
— Jesus

Possibly the greatest of *The Best Kept Secrets In The Kingdom* in the church today is an accurate understanding of the Kingdom of God. In this case, *The Best Kept Secret of the Kingdom* is the Kingdom itself!

Myles Munroe, in his book, *Rediscovering the Kingdom,* states, "The message of the Kingdom of God is the most important news ever delivered to the human race. Jesus came to earth to announce the arrival of this Kingdom and to establish it in people's hearts through His death and resurrection. As the Son of God, Jesus Christ was the exact likeness of His Father and represented Him perfectly on earth. To all those who believed in and followed Him, Jesus restored their citizenship rights in the Kingdom of Heaven and imparted His Spirit, so that they could represent Him and the government of heaven on earth."

Agreeably, the most important concept ever presented to mankind is that of the Kingdom of God. It is all Jesus talked about. Oh, sure He included hundreds of other issues, but everything He said and did, perfectly represented the Kingdom of God. He couldn't help it since He was the express image of God, Himself. If you want to know about the Kingdom of God, look at Jesus. Look at the things He did and how He did them; how He related to people; how he handled criticism and persecution; how He responded to the "religious" community; how He mixed with the poor and disenfranchised; how He trained His followers; how He handled seemingly impossible situations; look at all the ways in which He lived His life, and ultimately how He died and was resurrected from the grave. Look at the time He spent with His followers after the resurrection. When you look at Jesus, you can't help but see the Kingdom of God. Jesus both introduced, proclaimed, and demonstrated the Kingdom to mankind in his brief time here.

In his phenomenal book, *The Gospel of the Kingdom*, George Eldon Ladd writes: "The Kingdom of God is basically the rule of God. It is God's reign, the divine sovereignty in action. God's reign, however, is manifested in several realms, and the Gospels speak of entering into the Kingdom of God both today and tomorrow. God's reign manifests itself both in the future and in the present and thereby creates both a future realm and a present realm in which man may experience the blessings of His reign."

Matthew's account of the "good news" was clear in terms of what should be top priority; "Seek first the Kingdom of God and His righteousness, and all these things will be added to you." There's a good reason Jesus encourages us to seek the Kingdom first. It's because that's what's on the front burner for God, Himself. Our perspective on "every other thing" will be somewhat skewed until we begin to get a glimpse of His Kingdom. It's then, and only then, that everything else in life, religious or otherwise starts to come into focus. It's when, and only when, the Kingdom of God is given its rightful acknowledgment as "first" in everything that the true church begins to take shape.

The Kingdom of God is a vast subject. Some have spent a lifetime studying it only to discover they've barely scratched the surface. Don't get intimidated by that because as profound and vast as the Kingdom of God is, even a little child can begin to understand it! John the Baptist came proclaiming, "Repent, for the Kingdom of heaven is at hand." John was announcing, on God's behalf, that something new was bursting on the scene. It would be something so different and unique that would hold precedence over every other thing, living or otherwise. Upon the arrival of Jesus, the advancement of the Kingdom started picking up speed. His twofold purpose was to proclaim the Kingdom of God and to provide an entrance for all who desired to enter it. According to Jesus, that can only happen as a result of the "new birth" as he explained to Nicodemus, "You must be born again." At that point, we can begin to understand the things of the Kingdom. His Spirit will direct us and give His counsel at every turn if we'll just be sensitive to Him.

Again, Myles Munroe writes, "God's original purpose was to extend His heavenly rule to earth through human beings. His desire was that our physical earthly realm would reflect His spiritual, heavenly realm. Because the Kingdom of Heaven on earth was God's original and unchanging intent, it was also the focus of Jesus' message and ministry. The four Gospels together contain over 100 direct references to the Kingdom. John the Baptist preached the Kingdom. Jesus preached the Kingdom; it was His only message. Peter, James, John, and the other apostles preached the Kingdom. Paul preached the Kingdom. The early Church preached the Kingdom. A dark and weary world, hopeless and despairing, awaits—and desperately needs to hear—the good news of the Kingdom of God. By preaching the Gospel of the Kingdom to all nations, we prepare the way for the return of Christ. That is our mission, our assignment as the Body of Christ. If we do not preach it, who will?" (*Rediscovering the Kingdom*).

An integral part of our existence is to co-labor with Jesus as ambassadors in the advancement of His Kingdom. Since God owns everything, this Kingdom invasion isn't at all geographical. Much to the contrary; it's an invasion into, or over the heart of man. Totally unlike one nation overtaking another nation that traditionally does so through violence and warfare God's plan is to invade the hearts of mankind through His unconditional love and carried out only through His obedient sons and daughters. "Rejoice little flock; for it's the Father's good pleasure to give you the Kingdom." We've been given the Kingdom! Think about that! It's certainly not a thing we could've earned. It's only the result of a loving Father Who deeply desires that His children be included, and have a vital part in the most important undertaking in world history!

The Kingdom and the Church

The Kingdom and the church share a mysterious but beautiful and intriguing relationship. Some have erroneously concluded that the church and the Kingdom are one and the same. While that is clearly not the case, as the Kingdom encompasses all. The church still shines brightly and remains a critical component of the Kingdom in that it is the only organism entrusted by God with all the authority and power needed to articulate, assimilate and facilitate all the benefits of the advancement of the Kingdom on earth. In fact, it could be said that the church has power of attorney on behalf of the Father to carry out all the duties and facets of the Kingdom. Jesus said, "I will build My church, and the gates of hell will not prevail against it. And I will give you the keys of the Kingdom of heaven …." We (the church) have the keys of the Kingdom. By God's own design, He won't reach over the church to do what He has given us the authority and power to do! We are to move in cadence with Him ("in Him, we live and move and have our being") as the Kingdom is established on the earth.

For the Kingdom church to come into its own, two things need to be in place. First, it must be done with the right heart. Secondly, it must be done according to pattern. A great picture of this in the Old Testament occurred when David went to the house of Abinadab to reclaim the Ark of the Covenant. David, the apple of God's eye, definitely had the right heart. He was God's handpicked man to be the king over His people. David did the best thing he knew to do. He built a new cart to carry the Ark. Seemed innocent enough. On their way to Jerusalem one of the oxen stumbled. A man named Uzzah reached out his hand to steady the Ark to keep it from tumbling off the cart and he was stricken dead on the spot! Even though David had the right heart, he had the pattern wrong. Upon further investigation David discovered that God had given strict instructions in the Levitical Law as to how the Ark was to be transported. The Levites were to hoist the Ark with the poles made of acacia wood on their shoulders and carry it. David made the necessary adjustment and they proceeded on their journey. When the Ark arrived on Mt. Zion the glory of God fell, and remained. The lesson here: If we build with the right heart but wrong pattern, no glory of God; right pattern with the wrong heart, obviously still no glory. It's only when the right heart is coupled with the right pattern that the glory of God appears. Building the church in our generation should be done with the right heart having as its #1 priority building on true Kingdom principles. When that happens, we can expect His presence, His favor, and His glory.

> "There is a Kingdom mentality and mindset that bypasses and transcends the normal traditional church system mindset, which in many cases has become stagnant, outdated, and ineffective. This Kingdom mentality brings what much of the church has disregarded as"not for today" or relegated for someone else to do somewhere else (or postponed for a future time), and acknowledged those things as pertinent, vital issues for today; the Kingdom church is in the process of implementing them now. The greatest tangible evidence of this "Kingdom" mindset is LIFE! The church becomes ALIVE! Church life and ministry take on a completely different dimension with a Kingdom mindset. When the Kingdom is a priority, "life" is chosen over useless tradition and dead religion. So, from a Kingdom church's perspective, life is not optional. It is mandatory! The Church is to display the LIFE of the Lord Jesus Christ! In a Kingdom church, that kind of life will be evident in everything it does, and its people will reflect it."
> —AT

In Jack Taylor's book, *Cosmic Initiative*, which I recommend as the best entry-level book on the Kingdom, he states:

"Developing a Kingdom mindset begins with learning the nature of the Kingdom. The word Kingdom itself begs definition, especially in a democratic society where the term is seldom used and even less understood. Any Kingdom on earth includes three things: a king or queen, Kingdom citizens, and the principles that characterize the relationship between the two. Or, to put it succinctly, a sovereign ruler; those who are ruled; and "rules." The Kingdom of God has those same elements, but on the highest plane, and His Kingdom exemplifies His divine nature and character. There are many Kingdoms, but the Kingdom of God is one of a kind, and it is the only one that deserves the title "the Kingdom."

The DNA of a Kingdom Church

There are certain identifying characteristics of a Kingdom church. The list of those ingredients is not a particularly long one. Make no mistake about it; it's a very important list, especially as it relates to the formation and function of the church today. One needs only to look at the life and ministry of Jesus to get a clear glimpse into them. Some of these elements are important enough to warrant a chapter of their own later in this book. Following is a capsulized look into some of the more important ones.

A Kingdom Church Is Relational With the Father

I see it as the single most important issue in the formation of a Kingdom church. "You search the scriptures, for in them you think you have eternal life, but you're not willing to come to Me that you might have life." It was an issue in Jesus' day and even more so today. From God's perspective, it was intended to always be about the relationship! Leaders must first engage and interact in that relationship themselves and teach and impart the importance of it to their followers. It's only when we discover our extreme value as "chosen" sons and daughters of the Father that we begin to find our validation and significance, our purpose, and contentment. It's not enough to just know "about" the Father. We can do that by reading the Bible. We must "taste and see" that the Lord is good. We can only "know" Him by giving Him access to our lives.

A Kingdom Church is Learning to Interact As a True Biblical Family

The simplest definition of the church is a family. A Kingdom church is built on relationships; first with the Father then with one another. It's much harder to build on relationships because of all the obvious challenges involved, but the payoff is well worth the effort. The end result is a company of genuine people learning to love one another. It's something that those on the "outside" can sense. Whether they know what it is or not they're drawn into an organism that displays the agape kind of love. It (love) never fails!

A Kingdom Church is Growing in Its Expression of Agape

Scripture reveals that even if we have every other thing right but miss the "love" factor, we've committed an epic miss! Learning to love and allowing Jesus to love "through" us brings genuine life to the Body. There's no substitute for it. Giving grace to one another in all the affairs of life causes the church to be a beacon of hope in a dark world. A powerful atmosphere is created when people relate to one another with unconditional love.

A Kingdom Church Has Vision for the Future

"Without vision, the people perish." When Jesus began His earthly ministry, He knew what He was doing and "where" He was going. He was laser-focused in the things He did. After all, He was on a mission from the Father. In fact, He said, "I only do what I see the Father doing." As 21st century believers, we should have the same resolve. The Kingdom church, not unlike Jesus, has a keen sense of where to go, what to do, and how to do it!

A Kingdom Church is a Moving, Changing, Evolving Organism

When Jesus talked about the church, He wasn't referring to an organization, but an organism. Organisms by nature are made up of living cells. The church should be alive because of the presence of God in her midst, and its people who are being filled with the Holy Spirit. "Where the Spirit is, there is life"! As the church becomes more aware of the Kingdom of God change is inevitable. It's good change! It doesn't come without plenty of obstacles and challenges, though, which is true with nearly every form of life, but it causes the church to be a moving target. In reality, the church should constantly be evolving into a truer version of what it is supposed to be. Change is constant with a Kingdom church. Around here, we say, "Change is the new normal"!

A Kingdom Church Has a "One Church" Mentality

While there are many expressions of the Body of Christ, there's just one church! "In Christ, there's neither Jew nor Greek, slave nor free, male or female; we're all one in Christ." It's powerful, life-giving, and unifying when an individual or church begins to awaken to this.

A Kingdom Church is Committed to Prayer

Prayer for a Kingdom church is a non-negotiable issue. Personal prayer is one thing, but corporate prayer is fairly non-existent altogether in most churches. My experience has shown me that in many churches, it's not given much priority at all. Many of the results, or the lack of results, for any church can be directly traced to its commitment to prayer.

A Kingdom Church is a Worshiping Church

God is looking for true worshipers, and a Kingdom church makes worship a high priority. Understanding that the Lord "inhabits the praises of His people" is a key to a more tangible expression of His presence anytime the church convenes.

A Kingdom Church Has a Special Love for the Poor

There's no Biblical record or mandate for the government to care for the poor in our communities, but there's plenty of evidence for the church to do so. There is great potential in the poor in all our communities, and virtually no one is contending for them. One cannot escape the fact that if the Body of Christ is to do the work of Jesus in the earth, ministry to the poor cannot be ignored or overlooked.

A Kingdom Church is an Equipping Church

One of the most powerful adjustments any church can make is to equip its people for ministry rather than just teach or feed them. In reality, it's the only thing that causes the Body to take shape and be the church that's depicted in the Bible.

A Kingdom Church is Full of the Power of God

One of the most obvious manifestations of the presence of the Lord is the demonstration of signs and wonders. Everywhere Jesus went, miraculous events took place. He was clear that those who believed in Him and the works He did, they would do also. Much of the modern church is suspended between the miraculous things God used to do and the miraculous things they believe He will do sometime in the future. The Kingdom church acknowledges and believes those things should happen now! A powerless church won't make much difference in a darkening world. The power the Holy Spirit provides is just the thing needed to awaken the apathetic church to its purpose and destiny and to alert the world that there's something significant in the wind.

A Kingdom Church is Not Obsessed With End Times

Obviously, the study of end times is important. But an obsession of the subject is not healthy for anyone. There have been more than a few predictions, even in my lifetime, that Jesus was coming back soon. Some have even dared to put a date on it, only to be embarrassed by the sobering reality when it didn't happen. Scripture seems to be clear regarding the issue, "No man knows the day or the hour." Some seem puzzled at my urging to not to be obsessed with the end times. They ask, "Where's your urgency?" My urgency is doing *this*—seeking the Kingdom, implementing the principles in my own life and the church, and being busy in the things of God. From my observation, those who are obsessed with the end times are not doing much to change the world!

As broad a subject as is the Kingdom of God, Dallas Willard seems to have found a way of simplifying it in a nutshell.

> "The Kingdom of God is what God is doing. Both testaments use the word reign in this respect. The reign of God is the Kingdom of God. So what is the Kingdom of God? You need to know that or else you cannot "seek first the Kingdom of God," can you? So how do you seek first the Kingdom of God? Well, you would try to find out what God is doing and get involved with it."

There's another great quote by an unknown source that says:

> "Those who navigate at sea understand that neglecting small variants at the beginning of a journey can require serious course corrections later on."

It speaks to where much of the church is in our generation, where teaching and implementation of the Kingdom has been neglected. I have a strong opinion that there must be some serious course corrections refocusing on the Kingdom if the church is to be the glorious church the Bible describes. When an emphasis is put on the Kingdom, everything changes!

God Loves You, And There's Nothing You Can Do About It

There's not a truer statement. But there are millions out there who, for some odd reason, think differently. And to compound the problem, there's the over religious, self-righteous, doctrinal police, church guy telling everyone that God's mad at them. That's the result when people read their Bible but have no actual relationship with the Father. That person has no understanding of the grace of God.

I was talking to a friend that I hadn't seen in four or five years. He said that he'd been in a hard place. He blamed God for the death of his father and turned his back on Him. His exact words were, "God, just leave me alone." What he found after a few years of being mad at God was that the Father just loved him more! Somehow, He loved my friend back into relationship with Himself! That's the God that I know!

Have you been mad at God? I know a lot of people who have been mad at Him at one time or another. It's understandable. Some of them have been mad at Him for years. And for the most part, their anger has resulted from something they believed God mishandled. There's everything from, "God, why did you let my mom die?" to "Why do you make my life like it is?" What would you think if I told you that God can "take" that? He really can. In some strange way, I think He understands. After all, He made us! What's amazing is that He never ever lets that affect His love for you in an adverse way. Much to the contrary, I think it's like my friend experienced—He'll end up loving you more.

There's nothing you can do to diminish the Father's love for you one degree! You can be mad at Him; you can cuss Him. You can even tell Him you hate Him and turn your back on Him. He'll still keep on loving you, and there's nothing you can do about it!

This and more thoughts from Andy can be found at his blog:
"The Way I See It" - www.andyrtaylor.com.

PLAN OF ACTION:

- Make the Kingdom a priority
- Start now to "seek first" the Kingdom of God
- Choose one or more of the books listed to enhance your study
- Implement Kingdom principles into your life

LEADERS:

- Begin to slowly but deliberately incorporate Kingdom concepts into your church
- Learn to articulate the principles and values of the Kingdom
- Teach on the Kingdom—You'll learn more than anyone else
- Continue to make learning/teaching about the Kingdom part of everything you do
- Keep the Kingdom "central" in your theology and practice

PRAY:

"Father, help me to understand Your Kingdom."
"Help me to implement Kingdom principles in my life every day."

RESOURCES:

- *The Unshakable Kingdom and the Unchanging Person* by E. Stanley Jones
- *Cosmic Initiative* by Jack Taylor
- *Rediscovering the Kingdom* by Myles Munroe
- *The Gospel of the Kingdom* by George Eldon Ladd

One Church

"But now indeed there are many members, yet one body" (1 Cor. 12:20).
—Paul the Apostle

All who are born again are part of this mystical organism called the church. In Christ there's neither Jew nor Greek, slave or free, male or female; we're all one in Christ." It's a principle that Paul addressed numerous times in his letters. It appears that even in the first century, when the church was still in its infancy, there were already different factions vying for prominence. The church in Corinth presents a good case in point; Paul writes, "And I, brethren, couldn't speak to you as to spiritual people but as to carnal, as to babes in Christ. I fed you with milk and not with solid food; for until now you were not able to receive it, and even now you are still not able; for you are still carnal. For where there are envy, strife, and divisions among you, are you not carnal and behaving like mere men? For when one says, "I am of Paul," and another, "I am of Apollos," are you not carnal?"

Early in the life of Trinity Fellowship, the Lord woke me up in the middle of the night. I immediately heard Him say, "I want you to change the name from Trinity Church (a name that a very small group of people had arrived upon before we agreed to take the church in 1989) to Trinity Fellowship. I asked the Lord, "Why?" He said, "If I'm going to have a kingdom church in this region, I need someone who thinks like I do." The name change from "church" to "fellowship," which might seem like a trivial thing to some people, caused me to start thinking completely different about the "whole church" in our region. We started then to pray for the other churches and leaders in our town and area. That's been 30 years ago now, and we still pray for them on a weekly basis.

The last year on the ranch in Texas, I was enlisted by a man to take care and oversee 2500 head of cattle. My life was in a state of renewal. I was definitely ministry-minded by then but had no intentions, whatsoever, of ever pastoring a church. While in one of the large pastures overlooking the city of Canadian, Texas (town of 3000), the Lord impressed me to begin to pray over the city. I'd get in the back of my pickup, stretch out my hands over Canadian, and pray. I did this at least once a week in the summer of 1988. Fast forward 13 years.

We had started the small work in Sayre, Oklahoma, with only six to eight people and were experiencing slow, but steady growth. We had continued to pray for Canadian. We felt at that time that the Lord was telling us to plant a church there. We agreed to meet with the Ministerial Alliance in Canadian and tell them of our intentions. I was born in Canadian and at that time had lived in Hemphill County for 25 years. Donald Hill, our man to be pastor of the church was born there and had lived in Canadian his entire life. The longest any of these men in that Ministerial Alliance meeting that day had been there was about 4 years. The meeting was one of the most awkward and uncomfortable I've ever experienced.

I've never been treated so rude and disrespected since I've been in ministry. There was one man that kept pretty quiet, for the most part. I found out later that he called the pastor in our town from his denomination. He said, "These guys came to our Ministerial Meeting today and are planning to plant a church here. What about 'em?" The pastor in our town answered, "You need to welcome them into your town." The Canadian pastor questioned, "What do you mean? Why would we do that? We already have enough churches in town." This is the answer he received, "Because, if you'll welcome them into your town, every other church there will be better because they're there!" I was deeply touched by his response. I believe it's directly attributed to the fact that we have consistently and diligently prayed for all the churches in our area over the years. The "one church," kingdom mindset, and then praying accordingly destroys the competitive spirit that exists across the nation, especially in rural America.

Unity in the Church:

Unity is an important issue. The Bible gives many examples of the power and favor that only come through genuine unity. "If two of you agree as touching anything and ask it in My name, I'll do it." "Where two or three are gathered together in My Name, I'm there in the midst." It's easy to make the mistake that unity means that we all believe everything alike. That'd be great if it were true, but it just ain't so. In fact, it's very possible to discuss any one of the dozens of scriptural topics that are somewhat controversial and find that hardly any two of us agree 100% on any subject. So, just what does unity in the church consist of? For starters we must be unified in spirit. I believe that only comes as we continue to develop a kingdom mindset. The Holy Spirit is able to draw us together even when we might disagree on Biblical topics.

There are a few things we must agree on such as: Jesus is the Son of God; He was born of a virgin; He lived a sinless life; He died on the cross; He arose from the grave; He now sits at the right hand of the Father. Those things are non-negotiable issues if we're to walk together. There are hundreds of other things that we might not see eye to eye on, and that's OK. In fact, it could be a very good thing. Jordan Peterson, a brilliant clinical psychologist from Canada says, "We must assume in any conversation that the person sitting across from us knows something we don't." It's in some of those deep discussions about spiritual things that we learn to get our feet under us, so to speak, about what the Word actually says, and what we believe about it. I'm not for arguing Scripture; I don't think it holds much value. Discussion in a healthy atmosphere with an open mind can be a very good and life-giving exercise, as well as a profound learning experience. It's always a good thing to get another's viewpoint. A great quote by Aristotle gives some great wisdom: "It's the mark of an educated mind to be able to entertain a thought without accepting it." As believers, we're all on the same road, but in reality, we're also all on a different place on that road. In thinking and praying about unity awhile back, the Lord said to me, "When it stops being about you, you'll start to experience true unity." If you think about that, it works in a friendship, business partnership, in a marriage, and even in the church. As kingdom people, we should continue to make unity a priority but, at the same time, not be too demanding when others don't see things exactly like we do.

When we understand that our brothers and sisters in other churches and denominations have as much to offer as we do, we'll see them altogether different. You see, the enemy, who walks about like a roaring lion, comes at us unified in his attack. While in many cases in the church today we're arguing over who has the most people in church on Sundays! It's a sad but true fact. As our mindset changes to a more kingdom one we begin to shake off that ugly 'competitive' spirit in favor of a more unified and loving one. Then we understand that we're all working toward the same goal—the establishment of the Kingdom of God on the Earth. We should understand that we are just part of the Body. Therefore, we want to be a part of the Body that's functioning and doing our part while we diligently pray for all the other expressions of the church to do likewise. That's a kingdom mindset, and the Father loves it!

We're all an important part of the family of God. When we start acting like it, miraculous things are apt to happen!

A Place Where People Get Well

We started Trinity Fellowship back in 1989. Julie and I knew we'd heard the Lord about the work in Sayre. There was a little small group of about 8-10 people coming from the whole spectrum of backgrounds. Baptist, Church of Christ, Pentecostal, Charismatic....and a few who didn't know what they were, but just knew they wanted to go on with the Lord.

From the very start, it has been a place 'where people get well'! "Well, from what?" you might ask? Some of them get well physically; we've always believed in the miracle-working power of God. There's story after story of how the Lord defied all the doctor's reports, and someone was gloriously healed. It still isn't rare for me to ask someone, "How'd you find us?" and their reply, "I've got cancer and I heard God heals people here!" Some of them get well emotionally; Trinity has been a place where hurting people come. The word is out! Because of the "good news," there's hope for the hopeless. Some get well from the ill effects of dead, lifeless, and mean-spirited religion. There are droves of those people out there that have been plowed under by religion and religious people. Many will never darken the door of a church again. But a lot of those people give us a try, and you know what? They get well, too! Some get well from the clutches of addiction, others from heartbreak, grief, and lots of other things. It hardly ever happens overnight, but it nearly always happens!

We would never take the credit for it; They're not getting well because we're good at this stuff. People get well when they're loved. We don't have that perfected, but we're working on it. Anytime anyone connects relationally with the Lord, they stand a really good chance to get well. It's His love that makes the difference. Love never fails, you know!

It feels good to be known as a "place where people get well!"

This and more thoughts from Andy can be found at his blog: "The Way I See It" - www.andyrtaylor.com.

PLAN OF ACTION:

- Find the verses in the New Testament that confirm the "one church" view
- Begin to pray specifically for the other churches in your area by name
- Find out the names of their leaders and pray for them
- As you do this you'll notice that your heart will begin to change accordingly

- You'll learn that rejoicing at the little victories other churches may experience becomes a natural thing

LEADERS:

- Ask the Father for an ongoing revelation of the "one church" mentality
- Teach this principle to your people
- Pray specifically for the other leaders in your area
- Look for ways to participate as one church in your community
- Celebrate other churches victories with your people

PRAY:

"Father, thank You that You have called us all into one Body.
Help me to adjust my life with this new mindset.
Help me to have the correct heart toward other expressions
of the church in my area."

Building With Vision

"Where there is no vision, the people perish" (Prov. 29:18).
—Solomon

One of the first, and key ingredients of building any organism (or organization) that is effectual and relevant for the times and culture is the necessity of vision. Without vision, any entity, whether it be a person, business, or in this case, the church is destined to wander about aimlessly without getting much accomplished. All great leaders have vision and their work is a testament to that. It's the same with just about any successful endeavor; with vision, results are multiplied because everyone's working toward a common goal. Lee Iacocca is a great example of a leader with vision. Best known for the development of the Mustang and Pinto models for the Ford Motor Company he then stepped into leadership of the floundering Chrysler Corporation in the 80s and completely turned the company around earning a huge chunk of the automobile market share, worldwide. The momentum he ignited still exists today! That's just one example. There are hundreds of others but one of the key factors of virtually all of them is that they had a vision for where the company should go. It's a proven fact; people follow leaders with vision.

What is Vision?

I like to say that vision is the "roadmap" of where we're going. It is a declaration of an organization's goals and objectives intended to guide its internal decision-making.

The vision for your church could be 5-10 (there's no magic number) things that you believe are worthy of spending time, energy, and resources to accomplish. A clearly written, and communicated, vision helps everyone throughout every organization know their place and what they can do to contribute to the success of the business, church or project. It's a snapshot of the future, which may be a generation or more out there in front of us. If we know where we're going, everything we do today is strategically moving us toward our destination. Less time is wasted, and everyone's efforts are energized and maximized when there is vision. When everyone has a clear picture of where they're going, momentum picks up steam in a hurry. Vision is a concise collection of those essential elements that tell us, both generally and specifically, where we're going.

How do I Arrive at the Vision For My Church?

Here's where a business and a church might differ in the search for their vision. A great business leader might have some of those essential elements that are derived from their previous experience. There are things he has tried that worked and things that didn't work. With the church, there's only one way to arrive at a viable vision that will stand the test of time. I tell young leaders that they need to "go to the mountain." By that I mean they need to take a time of fasting and prayer getting away from the day to day busyness and get their focus entirely on the Lord. Oddly enough, even though I highly recommend that leaders go to the mountain that's not how I received the vision for our House at all. In the first few months of the life of Trinity Fellowship I began to jot down some things I believed the Lord was saying to me. I did this on a little yellow legal pad. They were things that looked and sounded too far fetched, and obviously way beyond my ability and experience. Although I prayed about these things almost daily I never showed or talked about them to anyone for several years. I was embarrassed to show anyone. I mean, how could a little rag-tag group like ours ever in a million years accomplish anything like this? It didn't look like anything was happening. But I still, somehow, believed they were from the Lord (See Trinity Fellowship Vision). I wasn't looking for any vision for Trinity at that point in time. I'm not sure I even knew anything about vision, or that it was even important, at the time. I just knew that these were things that seemed important enough for the Lord to reveal to me. At least that's where I thought they were coming from. 30 years later, those things are still important, and we're still progressing toward them. Yes, the vision for our House obviously came straight from the Lord! Arriving at, and then embracing a God-given vision is a non-negotiable issue for the church. If we're going to build anything significant, we must have the Father's wisdom and His perspective. If it's going to work, it has to be His plan. And if it is His plan, while it takes lots of effort and obedience on our part, it WILL work!

Vision = Provision

When we head out in the direction the Lord has directed, we can count on Him, bringing the necessary resources we need in perfect timing. Since it's His church, He's responsible to provide everything that's needed. We still need to be obedient. We still need to be diligent and responsible, but the Father will amaze you in how He provides for His church.

In 2000 Julie and I were in bed. She was asleep; I was in that place halfway between awake and asleep. I felt like the Lord said, "Someone is going to give the church a million dollars." Well, as you can imagine, that really got my attention, and I awoke fully. I immediately started to do what many of us do on a regular basis. I thought, "That was probably me, and not the Lord at all." In that very second, again, I felt like the Lord said, "You need to speak it out to give it life." Even though it was in that still, small voice it seemed pretty clear. I tugged on Julie's pajama sleeve and woke her up. "Julie, someone's going to give the church a million dollars." She said, "OK, good!" and went right back to sleep.

From that point, we began to do what I encourage others to do when they "think" they hear the Lord. We started to "say it, and pray it." To be honest, at the beginning, I didn't have much faith for it at all. As we continued to do that, my faith began to grow until nine years later, the oilfield activity in our area flatlined, the economy had dropped off dramatically. I got a call in the middle of the day. It was a friend we knew well, but he didn't even go to church with us at the time. He said, "Do you mind if I come by?" We went into my office and sat down around a small round table. A tear trickled down his cheek, and he reached in his pocket and handed me a check for a million dollars! I have often wondered what, if anything, would've happened if I had talked myself out of that when I first heard it nearly ten years before!

On another occasion, a friend of a friend was in our area, and my friend invited him to come by and look at our new building, which was in the final stages. We gave his friend the tour and as we stood in the lobby he reached in his pocket, handed me a check and said, "There'll be more where that comes from." I didn't even look at the check until he drove away. It was a check for a hundred thousand dollars! I just about had a heart attack! As incredible as the story is, this isn't even the best part. His friend was in the horse racing business. Before he drove off that day we prayed for him. One of the things we prayed was that he would be successful in that business and that the Lord would bless him back proportionally in what he had given us. This same man, several months later, had a horse that qualified for the Kentucky Derby. The odds on his horse were 50-1. His horse was so far behind for over half the race that it was embarrassing. He began to make his move and miraculously won the Kentucky Derby by several lengths. It stands as one of the greatest comebacks in thoroughbred racing history. There is a movie out about this man and the horse, Mine That Bird. The movie is, "50-1." You owe it to yourself to find the footage of that race on YouTube and watch it. You'll be amazed.

These are just a couple of actual stories (there are many others!) to validate that where there is God-given vision, there's always pro-vision!

Visionizing or "Casting the Vision"

Once the God-given vision has been established, it's extremely important to start the visionizing process. I call it "casting the vision." I sincerely believe that when a leader has been given directions by the Lord that those things are imprinted in his mind, will and emotions as well as in his spirit. The elements of that vision become "part" of you. In most cases a person who has it can't help but cast it because it's ingrained into your very being. That's exactly what needs to happen. You'll find that those closest to you will receive the vision the quickest, and they'll also understand it the clearest simply because they have heard your heart when you communicate it. The vision needs to be consistently communicated and referred to so that it will be at the forefront of people's minds. One challenge, especially in religious circles, is the fact that many people are very resistant to change of any kind. Following the vision puts the entire organism into a state of perpetual change. In casting the vision, it's important to let people know that "where we're going" is a much better place than where we are. The challenges are many, and resistance could be significant, but continuing to put the vision in front of the people is your guarantee that some, if not all, will eventually gravitate toward the goal. One thing we learned in the process of casting the vision here is that something truly supernatural happens when the vision is clearly communicated and put before the people in a variety of ways. We had talked about it for a few years, and people were receptive to it, for the most part. But it was when we hung a 6x6 foot framed picture with an eagle soaring over the mountains with the vision superimposed over it that things began to happen! Almost the moment we hung the picture, we started experiencing some amazing growth. It was apparent that what was happening was the vision was becoming even more clear to our people, and they were identifying with it. The vision was becoming "real" to the whole Family.

> *Then the Lord answered me and said: "Write the vision And make it plain on tablets, That he may run, who reads it. For the vision is yet for an appointed time; but at the end, it will speak, and it will not lie. Though it tarries, wait for it; Because it will surely come, It will not tarry."*
>
> Hab. 2:2-3

Casting the vision is a lifetime process. It's important to consistently communicate the vision so people can be informed and reminded of what's important and so that newcomers can catch the vision of the House and find their place in it as well. When everyone is equally informed, there is much less potential for disagreement and resistance.

The Vision is Generational

God moves generationally. He doesn't live in the constricts of time, so it's not as important to Him as we think it is to us. The vision the Lord gives will nearly always be generational in nature in that it can't be accomplished in one generation. It's meant to live on! We have entered our 30th year and I tell people that we're no closer to fulfilling the vision than we were when we started. You might innocently ask, "Well, how could that be since you're telling me how powerful having a vision is?" As you get faithful with what the Father has given you, He gives you more. That's a Biblical truth. So, as we have proceeded in the direction of the vision for our House hundreds, if not thousands of good things have been accomplished but because we've been faithful to what God gave us the vision has broadened. The further you go, the further you can see. It's clear at this point that the vision won't be fulfilled in my lifetime. That's a good thing. Our dream is that the next, and the next generation of our family members will come along and do what we've done but do it a whole lot better than we have. It's possible, and it looks like it's in full swing!

Transferring The Vision to the Next Generation

If the vision is indeed multi-generational, then somewhere along the way, it becomes necessary to begin to think ahead and how we will pass the vision on to the next generation. I would encourage that process to start as soon as possible, even if it might be years before it actually happens. Starting to pray about it NOW would be a great way to get the ball moving in that direction. We've now been doing that for over 15 years. I felt like I heard the Lord say to me many years ago, "I'm not judging (grading) you on what the church does in your lifetime. I'm judging you on what the church does after you're gone." That statement has caused me to adjust almost everything we do to what happens after my run is completed. Some of the practical things include teaching the youth and children the vision and values of the House. It's our mindset here that when it comes time for someone to take my place that we won't do the traditional thing and go "outside" and find someone to do the job. We believe that the successors to fill those spots in our Family will be raised up right here. It is, after all, a Family business! And who better to fill our shoes than those young people who have been raised up with our own vision and values. While this is a much more complex and detailed issue, suffice it to say that planning ahead is the best way to prepare to pass the vision to the next generation.

The Visionary

It's the way of the Lord to give the vision to one man. From personal experience He burns the elements of that vision into the heart of the person. Even though it may be years, even generations from materializing, it still feels real to that person. As a leader you don't "own" the vision; it belongs to the Father. It has been entrusted to you to foster, nurture, guard and protect. I remember the early years well. There were a number of clean-hearted, well-meaning people who had all kinds of ideas as to how we should build and proceed. I can only explain this way. It's as if the Lord puts a compass in leaders where the vision is concerned. When that compass is pulled too hard in either direction the visionary can feel it. It's his responsibility, no matter how good others' ideas are, to pull that meter back to "true north" to keep the vision on track. As a leader you'll have great pressure and plenty of opportunities to compromise where the vision is concerned. My advice, don't! Stay the course!

There's only "one" vision for the church. Any other form or variation of that vision from another person causes di-vision. Early on, you'll more than likely be accused of always having it your way. It can look like that. My answer to those people in the early days was, "I don't have the authority to do it my way; I sure don't have the authority to do it your way!" I would say that if I had done half the things that little small group wanted me to do in the beginning, we still wouldn't have 50 people. Although it's not a Biblical title, the person with the vision for the church serves as the CVO, Chief Visionary Officer. Communicating and fostering that vision should be high on his list of priorities. As others catch the vision, they too, can be very valuable in visionizing the entire Family.

Moving Your Church Off High Center

It's not unusual for an existing church without vision to find themselves "stalled out." Maybe you're reading this book and just now realized that your church doesn't have a well crafted vision or in some cases, no vision at all. That makes for a monumental challenge. It's do-able, but it's going to take time and some very strategic planning. It's a much longer conversation, but arriving at a God-given vision and implementing that in an existing church must be done in very small, gradual increments. People, especially church people, are very resistant to change of any kind. So proceeding slow, but deliberately is a must when moving a church off high-center. It's well worth the effort in the long haul but extremely challenging, to say the least.

Vision Drift

I happened upon this term in a Christian leadership email that I receive. Vision drift is what happens when a church has vision, but the vision is not focused on for one reason or another. Maybe the leader who initially had the vision has moved on. Maybe the church just settled in and stopped moving. At any rate, vision drift just means that the church has drifted away from the things that are important and are now just maintaining and in a stale state. It's a sad place to be, but it happens with churches all the time. Again, it requires re-communicating the vision and beginning to move slowly but surely. It's the, "Where we're going is much better than where we are." scenario. People who have been in a stationary place for a time don't like change, and it definitely requires change. Moving ahead slowly, but surely, is the plan that works best.

Summary

I often tell people, "If you look at what you think is the vision for your church, and it looks do-able, it might not be the Lord." God characteristically doesn't call people because of what they can do; more often than not, He calls them to do what they cannot do *(without the help of the Holy Spirit)! If we could do it, we wouldn't need Him! If your vision looks utterly impossible and you have no idea how it could be accomplished, it could very well be God! Don't get intimidated by the magnitude of what you think you're hearing from the Lord.

The Father has made us to desire to be involved in something much greater than we are. His plans for the church in our generation is such a thing. The writer in Proverbs says, "Where there is no vision [no redemptive revelation of God], the people perish; but he who keeps the law [of God, which includes that of man]—blessed (happy, fortunate, and enviable) is he." (Prov 29:18, Amplified Bible). That doesn't mean that if we don't have vision, we just die. It does mean, though, if we don't have vision (a roadmap) much of our time, energy, resources, and consequently, our lives are wasted. Vision gives people something to live for. It helps the leaders and followers know what to do and what not to do. In the final analysis, people don't necessarily follow great preachers, but they do follow those who have vision.

In my experience, building with vision is definitely one of *The Best Kept Secrets In The Kingdom.* It's a sobering thought to realize that most churches do NOT have a clearly defined, well-communicated, or well-articulated vision.

Night Vision

Night vision technology has been around for a good while now. Night vision devices were first used in World War II and came into wide use during the Vietnam War. The technology has evolved greatly since their introduction, leading to several "generations" of night vision equipment with performance increasing and price decreasing. The devices are used for a wide range of applications, including military gunners, drivers, and aviators.

You don't have to use much of your imagination to understand how much of an advantage of being able to see at night would be. Most of what we, the general public, have seen has been in the movies. The military has used this technology to their favor giving them a decided edge in nighttime maneuvers. There's no doubt about it, being able to see at night in the darkness is a big deal.

The Father has made provision for His kids, too, when it comes to being able to see in the darkness. In fact, it was in the dark of night that the Angel came to the shepherds to announce the birth of Jesus. When we're connected and growing in our relationship with the Father, we begin to get His own perspective about the world we live in and all it entails. I'm not trying to be the prophet of doom, but we're living in dark times. The political landscape in America is downright discouraging, whichever side you find yourself on. Christians are being routinely mocked, criticized and, persecuted right here in our own nation; A nation which, by the way, was founded on Christian principles and religious freedom.

It's a sign of the times. Many are calling this a "post-Christian era," and I don't think they're too far off base. Jesus, Himself, said it this way, "There'll be a time when people will seek to kill you, thinking they're doing God a favor." As the Christian community, we have brought some of that stuff on ourselves with our own arrogance and "holier than thou" attitudes. That's going to have to change!

But in these times of cultural, societal darkness, the people of God should be at the top of their game. We should be in fellowship with the Father so that we understand how to see and navigate in the darkness and help others do so. We should be the encouraging factor in a discouraging world. After all, the

> perspective we have as sons and daughters of the King gives us an edge that much of the world doesn't have.
> So, put on your night vision goggles, and get out there and make a difference!
>
> This and more thoughts from Andy can be found at his blog:
> "The Way I See It" - www.andyrtaylor.com.

PLAN OF ACTION:

- "Go to the mountain." Set aside a time for fasting and prayer for the Father to reveal His plans, direction, purpose, destiny, etc.
- Begin to articulate what you hear from the Father
- As you garner "buy-in" begin slowly to implement the facets of the vision
- Consistently communicate the vision in all you do
- Celebrate small wins
- Stay the course!

LEADERS:

- "Go to the mountain." Press-in to the Lord for His vision for your church/ministry
- Communicate to your people the facets of the vision
- Be consistent in casting the vision
- Celebrate milestones on the way
- Keep the vision fresh

PRAY:

"Father, give me Your vision for my life.
Give our leaders Your vision for the church.
Help us to walk out the vision You have given."

Building on Relationships

"In real estate, it's location, location, location; in the Kingdom of God, it's relationship, relationship, relationship!"
—AT

It's true. The church, in its very inception, was intended by the Lord to be an organism built on relationships. It's a family! I include it in *The Best Kept Secrets In The Kingdom* because, in modern times, it seems there are other priorities in the building, sustainability, and life of the church. Good preaching, great worship, comprehensive pastoral care, and other ingredients are all important in the grand scheme of building the church. When a priority is not placed on relationships, I fear we're missing the point altogether.

Jesus was relational and easy to interact with. It's primarily why He came to Earth in the first place; to show us all how easy it is to be in relationship with God. Jesus said He and His Father are "One." They are so in sync with one another that you can't tell one from the other. In fact, he says, "If you've seen Me, you've seen the Father." In His time on earth, He stayed in constant fellowship (maybe a better word would be, "union") with the Father. "I only say what the Father says." Again, He says, "The works I do are what I see the Father doing." Jesus' plan was to model the intimacy He had with His Father as a pattern we could follow to have that exact same relationship. Our relationship with the Father is easily the most important one we'll ever have. Even the Lord would agree that our relationships with one another are right on the heels of that in order of importance. At the end of our life, we'll realize it's not money, fame, or social status that has made our lives rich. We'll then see clearly that it's the relationships we've been blessed with that stand out as having brought lasting value and fulfillment to our existence. We should make the mental adjustment now and place a high value on our relationships so we can get the most out of this life He has given us!

Soon after God created man from the dust of the ground, He said, "It is not good that man should be alone." It appears here that God is giving us a glimpse into His own nature and personality. Now, I know God is all-sufficient, and He needs absolutely nothing to complete Himself. In this instance, He declares that man does, indeed, need someone so he won't be alone. Another way to interpret this verse is, "Man will do much better if he has someone." Someone to interact with; someone to share life with; someone to love, and to be loved by, in return. Could it be that in this scenario, God is also saying that He needs someone to be the object of His attention, provision, adoration, and love? I think very possibly so! You see, God doesn't just "have" love; He is love! Agape love, the special kind of love that God loves us with, is love of the very highest quality. Agape love gives and requires nothing in return. With no one to show and give that love to, it's destined to lie dormant and unexpressed in the heart of the Lover. We're created to be in relationship with the Father and with one another so love can be expressed and experienced.

> *"And they continued steadfastly in the apostles' doctrine and fellowship, in the breaking of bread, and in prayers. Then fear came upon every soul, and many wonders and signs were done through the apostles. Now all who believed were together, and had all things in common, and sold their possessions and goods, and divided them among all, as anyone had need. So continuing daily with one accord in the temple, and breaking bread from house to house, they ate their food with gladness and simplicity of heart, praising God and having favor with all the people. And the Lord added to the church daily those who were being saved."*
>
> Acts 2:42

There was an incredible thing happening in Jerusalem after the outpouring of the Holy Spirit. Let me set the stage. On the day of Pentecost, there were thousands of people in Jerusalem. Some were locals, but many had came there to celebrate the Feast of Pentecost. After the miraculous outpouring of the Holy Spirit and the subsequent move of God in the city, many people from those outlying areas did not go back home until some years later, after severe persecution came on the church. They stayed in Jerusalem to experience the blessing of the Kingdom of God in its purest form. Some moved in with other local families. In some instances, there were as many as 60 people living together in a single dwelling during that period. Now, there's an opportunity for some major relationship problems! In Jerusalem, during that time, there were at least 8,120 believers in just a short period of time, most of them new converts. (120 in the upper room; 3000 on the day of Pentecost; 5000 more a few days later). They had no Bible. There was no outreach team; no man called the pastor. Yet the Lord saw the church as safe enough an organism that He could "add to the church daily." Soon after that, the Bible records, "… and the number of disciples was being multiplied." There was phenomenal growth taking place in Jerusalem. The Holy Spirit was in charge. People were interacting with one another in a healthy, life-giving way, and everyone in the city, saved and unsaved alike, knew that something significant was brewing. There was obviously plenty of opportunity for relationship problems. Maybe the difference was their willingness to place a higher value on those relationships than we are accustomed to today.

When a church makes the decision to build on relationships, it will become quickly apparent where the enemy focuses his attack. He will do his best to cause problems between any and every relationship if he can. If we don't take steps to offset the attack we could end up being a casualty in this spiritual attack. The Bible gives some well laid-out steps we should take when we are offended. Months back the Lord began dealing with me about a weak spot in our church. I had noticed there was an unusual number of people coming to me expressing their heartbreak about relationship riffs they were having with someone else in the church. I gave them good counsel but it didn't cross my mind at that point that this is not how relational problems are to be dealt with in the Kingdom.

The Bible is clear that if we are offended we should go to our brother, the one who offended us, and try to work for a resolution. While I had eluded to those verses many times I had never done an extensive teaching on the subject. As a result we were not very good at restoration but it wasn't the people's fault. They hadn't been taught. One of our elders came to me after I did teach on the subject and said the Lord spoke to him clearly, "When you get this right then I will bring the masses to your house!" It makes sense. Why would he bring them only to be hurt or offended and with no clear plan of reconciliation. Our communities are populated with people who have been offended at church and many of them have decided never to go to church again. Incidentally, the Lord has proven Himself faithful, as He always does when we're obedient, to my friend's prophetic word. We're now having new people every week, and some that have left are returning. It's now a much safer place.

I met David VanCronkhite in Melbourne, FL, in 1998. Some would call it a meeting of "chance" but I would call it a meeting orchestrated by the sovereignty of God. It was at a small men's gathering of about 80-100 believers. We arrived during the worship time and the Lord immediately drew my attention to two men a few rows from the front in the small room. I knew was I was supposed to meet them. I felt that was a clear message from the Lord. At the first break I made my way to these two men and introduced myself. We "hit it off," so to speak, and quickly became friends and now over 20 years later I consider David Kula and David VanCronkhite among my best friends. It's just how God supernaturally arranges things.

At the time, they operated a ministry in downtown Atlanta called Blood n' Fire, a ministry to the homeless in an old pre-Civil War warehouse just a few blocks from the Georgia State Capital. At that time they were feeding nearly a thousand of Atlanta's homeless each day. I invited David out to be with us in Oklahoma for a week. I still remember those days as they were very timely and strategic for us. David's prophetic anointing brought a welcome confirmation of things we had been hearing from the Lord for some time. After that week, as we drove the 2 hours back to the Oklahoma City Airport, David got very serious with us as he said, "For ten years we've been doing everything we know to do to build community and family with the homeless in Atlanta. You guys have it going on here at a degree we've never even seen before, and you don't even know it's happening!" Which says that it was nothing we orchestrated at all; it was clearly a profound work of the Lord! David saw people relating and interacting with one another in a loving, life-giving way that should be typical of a Kingdom family. Even though we were living it and experiencing it, it took someone from the outside to awaken us to its significance. We weren't smart enough or spiritually savvy enough to do it on our own, but God took our willingness to be relational and did something extremely valuable with it.

Since that time, we have been much more intentional about relationships and have done a better job of fostering that idea and model with many other individuals, churches, and ministries.

The Solution for Damaged or Broken Relationships

God is sovereign when it comes to relationships. By that, I mean, we only know the people we know simply because God wants us to know them. He orchestrates these relationships knowing that you have something the other person needs, and vice-versa. The other person has things that you need. In that way we help "complete" one another. When you look from that perspective and see the people in your circle of influence it becomes crystal clear that the Father did nothing less than a chain of miracles in all our lives to bring us into relationship with our family, our spouse, our friends and our acquaintances. If He has gone to that much trouble to do that it makes sense for us to put as much priority on our relationships as He has. It doesn't take long to figure out that in every relationship, given enough time, there are problems. If you don't believe me get in a car with someone and take a week-long trip across the country with them. Soon, some of the things the other person says and does starts to grind on you a little bit. Before long they're getting on your nerves. It works the same with them. Our culture has taught us that if we get offended, hurt or betrayed that we just scrap the relationship and move on to another one. Happens all the time. Get crossways with your boss, get another job. Have an argument with a friend, forsake the relationship for other friends. Having trouble with your spouse? Divorce this one and get another. Anytime we make the problem more important than the relationship, the relationship is in jeopardy. Sadly, this is the norm in our world today. People are suffering because of it. Nobody wins but even more important the Kingdom of God suffers too. It's a really bad witness to the world for the church. We, as Kingdom people should be better than this!

While the solution is simple, it's amazing the number of people who still won't do it. Here's how it should work.

1. Let's put the same value on the relationship that God has.
2. Because God put us together we must make the relationship more important than the problem! In fact, I think we need to use the same theory and mindset that God has used with marriage—"What God has joined together, let not man put asunder."
3. Let's sit down at the table with our hearts set on reconciliation. Invite the Holy Spirit. It might be a good idea to get a mediator to help you through the process.
4. Lets work through the issues. Apologize where it's needed. Own your issues. Learning to say, "I'm sorry, "I was wrong," or "I forgive you" are all very good things, and they help to bring healing and restoration.
5. The payoff = For those who are committed to reconciliation, they soon find that the Lord not only restores the relationship but restores it and makes it stronger than it was before the problem!

We've been learning to live by this example for 15-20 years now. We're still far from perfect, but we have seen some amazing healing happen in relationships in what would have otherwise been a hopeless situation! The Father loves reconciliation! When you decide to work at it, you'll have all the resources of Heaven on your side. Until you're willing to fight for the life of your relationships, your church or ministry is not a safe enough place for the Lord to bring the numbers. While it's not easy walking through offense, betrayal, and hurt feelings, we know we should do it anyway. The sad part is, most don't. If the church is going to be what He's destined her to be, that has to change. An "agape" culture evidenced by people working through the issues is the answer!

Some of life's greatest challenges and frustrations come through our relationships. It's worth it if we're willing to work for reconciliation! Someone said, "All relationships go through hell, real relationships get through it." In the final analysis, the church will only be as strong as the relationships it consists of. Any person or church that places as high a value on relationships as the Lord has will definitely be blessed as a result. To work through the issues and have a strong resolve for reconciliation is one of the *The Best Kept Secrets In The Kingdom*

Of All The Ways He Blesses Us

If you start to count up all the ways that God blesses you, you'll quickly find that the list is almost endless! He's not limited in the ways He blesses, and He seems to stop at nothing in His mission to show us just how much He loves us. Even some of His most hardened critics, if they were to be totally honest, would have to admit that He does this kind of thing on a routine basis. He doesn't just love us because He has to; He doesn't just love us because it's the 'right' thing to do; He doesn't just love us because we need it; All that may be true, but that's not why He does it. No, He loves us like we love our own kids (and grandkids!) He just can't help it!

His interaction with us is always motivated by love. Even in those times when we are receiving correction from Him, it's always in love. The Father doesn't just "have" love; He IS love! And every single thing He does or has ever done is for our benefit and well being. I'm grateful for good health. I've rarely been sick in my entire life. Oh, I've got plenty of aches and pains from some of my previous lifestyle choices, but all in all, I've been really blessed with good health. There are dozens of other things I could mention.

When I think of all the ways He's blessed me, my mind immediately goes to my family, then my friends and the people who I've met, and gotten to know, along the way. So, of all the ways He's blessed me, one of the things I'm the most grateful

> for is the people He's brought into my life. At the end of our earthly run, we'll see it clearer than ever. The things that have made our lives rich are not fame and fortune or some other empty thing like that, but the people we've encountered, day-in and day-out, on the journey of life. So, I'm suggesting we make the mental adjustment now and put a premium value on our relationships so we can enjoy our lives to the fullest, starting today!
>
> Thank you, Lord, for the people you've brought across my path!
>
> *This and more thoughts from Andy can be found at his blog: "The Way I See It" - www.andyrtaylor.com.*

PLAN OF ACTION

- Notice the people in your circle of influence
- Awaken to the fact that God has sovereignly arranged these relationships
- Place a high value on your relationships
- Learn to enjoy the presence of these people
- Interact as the Lord leads
- Be willing to work through any difficulties that might arise

LEADERS:

- Teach on the vital role of strong relationships in your church
- Set the example in your own relationships
- Be a "peacemaker" and teach your people to do likewise
- Develop a culture of reconciliation
- Reach out to those who have been hurt through their relationships
- Teach your people to be unoffendable
- As your church grows, you'll need to get more creative in encouraging people to be relational

PRAY:

"Father, help me to be aware of the sovereign relationships You have arranged. Help me to put the same value on my relationships that You have."

Equipping the Saints

"He has given some to be apostles, some prophets, some evangelists
and some pastors and teachers; for the equipping of the saints
for the work of the ministry, for the edifying of the Body of Christ,
till we all come to the unity of the faith ...."
—Paul

One of the most glaring omissions in the modern church is its failure to awaken to the importance of the above Scripture. When one is puzzled about why the church sometimes seems so ineffective, and its participants bored, and without direction, he needs to look no further than this one important topic. Equipping the saints obviously belongs on the list of *The Best Kept Secrets In The Kingdom*.

One might wonder how Paul could be so clear in his letter to the Ephesians of how ministry on a large scale (or small scale for that matter) should work and how it has been so neglected during modern times. There are several good, but not valid, explanations for the current state of ministry in the church today. For starters, most of 21st century Christendom has all but ignored the five-fold ministry, listed above, altogether. Sure, there has been plenty of talk about pastors, evangelists, and even teachers. The ministry of the apostle and prophet have been met with almost total disregard in the modern church. In fact, in most Christian circles today, you'd be considered an outright heretic if you were to openly declare the validity, or even the need, for apostles and prophets. Dangerous mistake, in my opinion. In fact, the Word even states that the ministry of the apostle and prophet is the foundation of the church, with Jesus Christ being the Chief Cornerstone. The omission of the ministry of apostle and prophet has caused the church to be much less effective in its function, and therefore in its results than it should be. That ineffectiveness is not seen any more clear than in the lack of personal ministry equipping for every believer.

Paul does such an eloquent and easy to understand teaching on the Body (1 Cor. 12) that one cannot escape the simplicity of the truth. In essence, we're all "body parts" in this mystical organism known as the church. We all have certain gifts and talents meant to enable us to be functional contributors to the "whole." When one or more of those Body parts isn't working, which is the case in most of the church, it profoundly affects the overall working of the Body. In most cases, it's because no one has told the people that they have a vital part to play in the health and activity of the church. As a result, ministry is left to only a willing few, and it has become the norm in nearly all of the church today. The result: A Body with only a few of the "needed" body parts working.

The fivefold ministry influence is best described as "gifts of men and women to the Body of Christ to equip individuals for the work of the ministry." The apostle has the God-given ability to set the church in order according to the will and purpose of God. The prophet both foretells of things to come and forth tells what the Lord is saying NOW so the church can make strategic adjustments to enhance its mission and success. The evangelist has a heart for the lost, to see them converted, and the anointing to train all members of the Body to be evangelistic in their normal daily routines. The pastor, or shepherd, is anointed to care for the flock by leading them, tending to them, and nurturing them toward their destiny. The influence of the shepherd causes that same care and concern to be contagious throughout the entire Body. The teacher, likewise, has a strong anointing to teach as well as equipping Body members to do the same. This is a general overview of how it should work. A more detailed explanation of the fivefold ministry is described later in this book.

The ministry mindset that exists in most churches today is one where, in most cases, the Pastor is saddled with nearly all the ministry. However, there are some more progressive churches where a few others help shoulder some of the duties and responsibilities. It's a rare occurrence to find a church in the process of equipping its people. Church folks are conditioned today to think that all ministry happens, or should happen, at church. Some of it should happen there, no question. But not all.

We must start looking at this differently! In most cases, it takes an abrupt paradigm shift for most people.

I'm a big fan of college basketball. It's about the only sport I can enjoy and not really care what teams are playing. There's a four to five point difference between teams that win the national championship and one that might not even make the NCAA Tournament. I'm as interested in the coaches strategy as I am in the game. A great coach is fun to watch. A few years ago, watching March Madness, the Lord started to show me that our Sunday gatherings at church should be like the time-out in a basketball game. Most good coaches, especially in a tight game, are strategic with their time-outs. In a big game, it's rare for the game to end with either coach having any time-outs remaining.

The game is not won during the time-out. In fact, there's not a single point scored during that time. However, the things that take place during that time-out have an extremely important part in the outcome of the game. In that time-out, players are encouraged; they're given specific instructions for their offensive and defensive strategy; the coach makes sure they're all clear as to what each player should do; they get unified as a team and go back in the game with a clear plan in mind. That's what should happen at church! Again, while there's plenty of ministry to happen on Sunday, the real "game" is outside the walls of the church.

People need to make the mental shift that they're not coming to church to be "fed," but they're coming to get equipped! It's not a rare thing for any leader to hear the criticism, "We're not getting fed." Agreed, leaders need to put in the time to preach and teach quality lessons/messages. Experience has taught me that most of those complaining about not being fed, don't do much with what they are fed! While babies need to "be fed," adults (mature believers) feed themselves. In an atmosphere where people are constantly needing fed and not doing anything with it is the equivalent of a person constantly stuffing themselves with food but not getting any physical exercise and becoming fat, lethargic and overweight. That's often the case with a church full of people wanting to be fed and not being equipped. We're to be "doers" of the Word and not hearers only!

Dealing with Resistance and Apprehension

It's a "given" that if it hasn't been communicated before, people will naturally be somewhat resistant to this new mindset. After all, in the minds of most church members today, other, more qualified people should be doing all the ministry and not them. That makes it clear why Paul wrote in such simple terms when describing the Body and how it should work. It's very simple when you look at it (the Body) as compared to a physical body. If they haven't been taught, it'll still be foreign to them. We're all put here to be ambassadors of the Kingdom of God. We've been given the authority and power to "right" every wrong we encounter in the course of our lives.

If people are going to start the process of stepping out in ministry, there needs to be easy entry levels for them to do so. One way that seems to work well for us is during our ministry time on Sundays. I might have those who have a need to be healed physically to stand, or maybe just raise their hand. I will then instruct anyone who doesn't have their hand up to go to the nearest person who does and lay hands on them. I usually give them permission to pray for those people if they are comfortable in doing so. I will still pray from where I am just in case no one around a person feels OK to do it. This is the analogy the Lord gave me: If you were working in your shop and accidentally cut your arm, immediately the healthy cells around the cut would rally around the cut to start to bring healing to your arm. When people go from where they're seated or standing in the church, to a person with their hand up, that's the equivalent of the healthy cells in the Body rallying around the damaged body part to help bring healing. There are other ways to give people an easy entry-level into ministry, and it helps to remove the fear and apprehension of ministry that most people experience. Most don't have any idea what to do. Leaders must lead the way. We must teach, and demonstrate how ministry should look. Jesus had a unique way of doing this; He first took the twelve with Him. He did the ministry and they watched. Then He let them do the ministry and He watched and critiqued them when needed. It was never done in a criticizing way but always nurturing, encouraging and life-giving. Soon He sent them out two-by-two with instructions on what they should do. His method still works today. When you or those who are getting experienced in ministry go on a ministry opportunity, take someone with you, preferably a novice that's willing. Don't demand that they do anything; don't put them in an uncomfortable situation; just let them watch. It won't be long before they'll begin to get more comfortable in doing the same. I've started asking after my messages, "What's your takeaway from the message today?" That helps people start thinking about their own ministry opportunities and how they might use the new information with their family, friends, or people they come in contact with. The added benefit is that your people will find themselves actually growing, maturing, and moving toward their destiny!

Bear in mind that Paul's letter written 2000 years ago to the saints in Ephesus, who were primarily new believers and some just coming to terms with their own salvation and spirituality. One might question "how" were they to process this new information of how ministry should take place. For starters, they didn't have a lot of useless church tradition to deal with like we do in modern times. I've been teaching these verses about equipping the saints for 30 years, and I'll be the first to tell you that because of perceived expectations of how ministry should be "fleshed out" the message must be consistently repeated over the course of time for some to catch it. Again, religion stands in the way! Be aware that what you already know, or at least think you know, can keep you from receiving more of the truth about any subject! If the fledgling believers in Ephesus could get it, so can you! But you need to start now to think different and in a more scriptural way.

The Holy Spirit will help you and your church just like He did for them. My phone rings less now than when we had 25 people! People are understanding that they can do the ministry, too! That's what happens when you start equipping the saints for the work of the ministry!

It's easy to see why the issue of equipping the saints qualifies as one of *The Best Kept Secrets In The Kingdom*.

I Plant a Little, I Water a Little

I was having a conversation with a pastor friend a day or two ago. We were having a good laugh about a few of those times when we were preaching or teaching, and it just wasn't happening, if you know what I mean. It's funny now, but at the time, it was not funny at all. One of those times for me was about 15 years ago. We were still in the old building and doing two services. It was the first service, and there were 50+ people there. It was one of those mornings that nothing was working. I had notes and was doing my best to teach from them, but it was just flat. To be honest, I wasn't making any valid points. What I was trying to teach wasn't making any sense, even to me! I'm tellin' 'ya, it just wasn't happening! In fact, I went into the sound room after the service was over and said to the guys, "If anybody got anything out of that, it had to be the Lord!" I was certain that nobody DID get anything out of it! I was relieved when the service was over so we could all be out of our misery! I would've like to have just gone home, but I had another service to do, and that'd just be awkward! (LOL)

A person came to the sound room, and I could tell he wanted to talk to me. I ignored him as long as I possibly could. I totally expected him to say, "WTH was that??!!" But he didn't. On the contrary, he said, "Man, that was really, really good!" I had two thoughts rolling around in my mind: 1) he's gotta be joking; 2) if he's really serious (which I couldn't imagine!)...I'm thinkin', "Was I there?!"

This isn't the only time this has happened down through the years. I wish it was. But those times it did happen, there were the same results nearly every time. Those times when I felt like I did my very worst would inevitably be the times that I would have the most people comment on how good the teaching was. I think the Lord likes it when that happens. What I've learned from those times is that it's just a little reminder from the Lord that everything doesn't necessarily depend on how 'good' a job we did teaching. Don't get me wrong; I want to continue to get better at teaching the Word. But in the final analysis, it's the anointing (supernatural blessing) of the Lord that's the deciding factor of whether it's actually good or not. He definitely doesn't want us to get prideful about how good we think our teaching is.

> We can plant; we can water. If anything significant is going to happen, it'll have to be the Lord that gives the increase!
>
> *This and more thoughts from Andy can be found at his blog: "The Way I See It" - www.andyrtaylor.com.*

PLAN OF ACTION:

- Decide to be equipped
- Take notes as you're hearing the message at church
- Think about how you could apply that in ministry opportunities that come your way
- Get comfortable praying for others for their needs
- Learn to follow the lead of the Holy Spirit
- Remember: it's not your ability you're relying on, it's His

LEADERS:

- Teach the Word concerning equipping
- Reinforce it often
- Give them easy entry levels into ministry
- Help your people find their passion
- Encourage your people to "step out" in ministry
- Affirm them when they do
- Critique them in a positive, life-giving way if needed

PRAY:

"Father help me to stay in a mode of being equipped and to find my place in the Body. Lord, Open doors of ministry for me."

Contending For Signs And Wonders

> "Most assuredly, I say to you, he who believes in Me,
> the works that I do he will do also; and greater works
> than these he will do, because I go to My Father" (John 14:12).
> —Jesus

It's really been mind-boggling to me over the years as to how many there are in the church today that deny the validity of signs and wonders. Many say all that passed away with the apostles. People in that group don't even ask for miracles nowadays! Others have been in a religious environment where they believe, but they believe it's happening somewhere else with someone more spiritual than them. The Father never intended for the church to be powerless. Now, in a time when the world needs to see the power of God in the worst way possible, signs and wonders MUST be included on the list of *The Best Kept Secrets In The Kingdom*.

Why Signs and Wonders?

For starters, since we're Kingdom people who have been given the mandate from Jesus to "right" every wrong we come in contact with in this life, signs and wonders serve to rearrange things like they're actually supposed to be from Jesus' perspective! Jesus said, "These signs will follow those who believe: In My name, they will cast out demons; they will speak with new tongues; they will take up serpents; and if they drink anything deadly, it will by no means hurt them; they will lay hands on the sick, and they will recover" (Mark 16:17-18). This was after the resurrection and immediately before Jesus ascended into Heaven to sit at the right hand of the Father. Mark closed out his letter by saying, "And they went out and preached everywhere, the Lord working with them and confirming the word through the accompanying signs" (Mark 16:20).

One of my favorite Bible stories is when John the Baptist was in prison. He sent two of his disciples to check Jesus out. They asked Jesus, "Are you the Coming One, or do we look for another?" Jesus was so confident and at peace with "Who" He was that He answered this way, "Go tell John, the blind see, and the lame walk; the lepers are cleansed, and the deaf hear; the dead are raised up, and the poor have the gospel preached to them" (Matthew 11:2-5). Jesus obviously had nothing to prove to anyone, but His answer was one that validated the Kingdom of God. It was being established and advanced through everything He did. The works Jesus did were enough for John to know, He is the One!

The Kingdom of God is not "just" about signs and wonders, but the signs, wonders, and miracles are evidence the Kingdom is working like it's supposed to be working! Signs and wonders confirm the word(s) and actions of Kingdom people. Miracles cause even unbelievers and skeptics to be convinced of the reality, the goodness, and the power of God!

I've written an article for a newspaper in a neighboring town for 15 years or more. One particular article was on the subject of signs and wonders. Another person who was obviously of "another" religious persuasion on the subject bought a quarter-page ad in the paper for two weeks running to refute what I'd written in my article. He addressed my article point by point detailing why my content was unscriptural from his perspective. In his ad, he was very critical, not only of what I'd written but leveled much of the criticism toward me, personally. Some of the people in my circle were concerned how I would react to the kind of public criticism I was getting. To be honest, it didn't really bother me since I had been the target of quite a few others through the years. I don't particularly like that kind of public attention, but I learned early on when you decide to be obedient to the Father and become a threat to the enemy, he has to find a way to try and discredit.

I was in a coffee shop in town and a man who had been to our church only a few times but had obviously found his home with us was there getting coffee. He was an oilfield worker and talked really loud even to the point everyone in the coffee shop couldn't help but hear what he was saying. He said, "Hey, you know that guy that wrote that article against you in the paper?" "You know, he's exactly right!" I immediately wondered where he was going with the conversation. I sure didn't want to get in a debate with the whole coffee shop hearing. Again, he said, "Yeah, he's right!" "He says there ain't gonna be no miracles, and he's right!" "The Lord ain't gonna do no miracles around that guy!" It's the truth; with anyone, anywhere who's intent on declaring there are no miracles today, it's a self-fulfilling prophecy. There will be NO miracles around them!

An interesting (and kind of funny) side note to this story; Normally, when I would email the articles to the newspaper, I'd send them in a batch of maybe 10-15 articles at a time. This particular batch had been sent at least five weeks before. After his first rebuttal of my article on signs and wonders, my next article (sent weeks before and not knowing he was going to attack them) looked like I had addressed every single thing he had said in his first ad! We were all amazed by that. I even had a few people in our circle thinking I had written the next article to get in a back-and-forth public battle of words with him. (which is not my style at all!) I had no idea when I sent the articles to the newspaper he was going to come back at me like he did. The Holy Spirit knew! I've learned in situations like this one I just need to stay the course and let the Lord sort it all out.

About fifteen years ago, the Lord said to me, "I want you to give away everything I've given you." I didn't know exactly what the Lord was talking about, but in innocent faith, I said, "OK!" Since that time, there have been countless miracles in our "circle." What has been equally amazing is that it's not just me and a few of our leaders operating in signs and wonders. It's the whole household! Our family is faithful to believe for miracles in what would normally be depressing, discouraging and even some impossible-looking situations. It's not limited to just an elite few; it's a family anointing. It's something the Father wants for every church!

On a Sunday when I was out of town, one of our couples brought their little two-year-old grandson with them to church. He had been born with severely bowed legs. They were so deformed his little pull-up diapers had to be cut on the sides and re-taped to even get them over his tiny legs. They brought him to the altar for prayer that morning. A couple days later he woke his grandparents up in the middle of the night a couple of times to rub his legs because of the pain. He woke up the next morning and his legs were perfectly straight! We had before and after x-rays to prove that this was an outright miracle. Even the doctors agreed. They brought him back a few weeks later and we stood him up on the communion table at the front to let people see how correct his little legs were now. That's a real faith-builder for a church, and it stokes the fire for the supernatural in everyone who witnesses. When someone believes for miracles, and it happens, it's contagious! Everyone wants to be involved, and that's exactly what the Lord wants to happen.

I was in a connected church in Tonto Basin, Arizona, for a series of meetings there. At the time of invitation I invited anyone who needed healing to come forward. A lady in her 50s came with a friend. I could tell she was very apprehensive about coming forth at all. I'm convinced she wouldn't have come down at all without the urging of her friend. Her friend did the talking. "She had a car wreck nine years ago, and she barely survived." "She had several broken bones, but since the wreck, she hasn't been able to lift her left arm above her waist." I asked her if it was OK for me to pray for her. She agreed. After I prayed I asked her to lift her arm. She said, "I can't." I said, "Lift your arm!" Again she said, "I can't!" I got louder and even more forceful, which isn't my style at all. I just felt the Holy Spirit leading me to do so. Again, in a loud voice I said, "Lift your arm!" "I told you I can't!" "Lift it now!" I said. She started trying to lift her arm and miraculously she raised it, but only a few inches above her waist. I said, "Lift it more!" She started to lift her arm and miraculously she had lifted it about shoulder high. "Keep going!" By now she was catching the reality that something miraculous was happening. She kept raising her arm until she held it straight up toward the ceiling. She was crying happy tears and screaming, "My arm, My arm!" "It's healed!" "I'm healed!!" It obviously got the attention of everyone in the meeting, and everyone agreed a miracle had occurred.

This is just the thing the Lord wants to do. "Where two or three are gathered together in His name, He is there in the midst." Where He is, and if and when we'll cooperate, these things can become commonplace.

We're located two hours west of Oklahoma City, only 25 miles from the Texas state line. When someone gets a serious report from their doctor they're routinely referred to a specialist in Oklahoma City who might be better suited to treat them. We've been amazed over the years at how many times someone gets a bad report here of something extremely serious, with some even being potentially terminal. Many times there have been x-rays revealing their obvious physical problems, only to arrive in OKC and finding out there's no problem at all! This has happened over and over throughout the years to the degree that we now expect it. We keep believing for signs and wonders, and the Lord just keeps doing them!

A lady had started attending our church, who Julie and I soon became close friends with. Her husband, a cowboy, gruff and rough around the edges, wasn't willing to come. She had asked me a few times if I'd come out and visit with him. (I'd never met him) This was something I really didn't want to do. I'll explain why; if someone wants to talk, I'm all over that! Just making one of those, let's say, "cold calls," I don't really like those because it kind of feels like someone has put a "contract" out on the person. They may not want to visit with a preacher at all. I'm not the "pushy" type, so I'll usually say, "No" to those requests. She was such a special person to us I finally, reluctantly said I'd do it. I went to their house in the country. I sat down at the kitchen table waiting for him to come in from the outside. When he did come in, we introduced ourselves, and he immediately said, "I'm gonna tell you right off, I don't like churches, and I don't like preachers!" I said, "Really, neither do I!" (which is not the truth at all, but it did give us a common point to start our conversation) It caught him totally off guard! From that point it was amazing how well we "hit it off!" We became great friends. Along the way he started having health issues. He was a hard worker but found that he had no energy. He'd try to get out and work and would get so tired he could hardly make it back to his house. Long story short, he was soon diagnosed with leukemia, and it was bad! Hospitalized in Oklahoma City for an extended time and not responding well to treatment, it became a very discouraging time for him. Daryle Perry, my best friend and right-hand-man for years, and I went to see him in the hospital. It was probably the worst day he'd had. The doctors, just that morning, had given him a 5% chance of living. We had a short visit with him as he didn't have the energy even to talk much. We prayed over him and asked the Lord for a miracle. To be honest, I wasn't very optimistic, but we prayed anyway. To everyone's amazement, especially the doctors, he was totally healed from leukemia! He was out of the hospital in no time living a normal life. He told me later that after we prayed for him that day, he never had another single thought of dying. He has since gone on to Heaven with something totally unrelated to leukemia. It taught me that even if I'm a little intimidated at the state of someone's condition, God is not! Pray anyway! See what God will do!

One of the most precious gifts the Lord has given our House is to pray over those who have not been able to have children. In nearly all these cases, the couples have gone through just about everything possible, medically, and still have not been able to conceive. There have been at least twenty and maybe as many as thirty of these cases over the years that after having exhausted every possible solution with the doctors, only to end up discouraged, they came to us for prayer. There are now little kids everywhere who are a direct result of a miraculous touch from the Lord!

We had a church connected with us in Juarez, Mexico. A team of us were there for a series of meetings. A couple from Phoenix found out we were going to be there. They had been trying to get pregnant for a few years but to no avail. They drove all the way from Phoenix to get prayed for. They were there for just one night and turned around and went home. We got an ecstatic call from them three months later saying they were pregnant and expecting a little boy! He's now ten-years-old!

Another couple who had tried everything medically came and had us pray over them. They didn't have a baby. They had two!! That miraculous set of twins are now 12-years-old. I see them on a regular basis, and I can't help but express my gratefulness to the Father again for His faithfulness and miraculous power.

A funny story; one of our couples that was NOT trying to have kids found out they were going to be parents again. It was quite a surprise for them as they already had three kids and by this time, they weren't as young as they once were. Upon finding out she was pregnant she told her husband. He was shocked and kind of scolded her, saying, "What did you do?" "Did you go down there at church when they were praying for people to get pregnant?!" He got OK with it pretty quick, and now they have a little boy that's eight. So, now when we're praying for those having a hard time getting pregnant, we jokingly tell people to stay out of the "zone" if you don't want to have a baby!

Another couple had been trying to have a baby for several years. They were getting to the age where it was questionable whether they should get pregnant or not. We prayed over them, and they did get pregnant! In a few short months, the mom miscarried. As you can imagine, they were devastated, especially after going through not being able to have children, then miraculously becoming pregnant. It was a tough time we walked through with them. I struggled myself, wondering how that could've happened, knowing the pregnancy was orchestrated by the Lord. Fast forward another year; she became pregnant again. They now have a little girl six years old! We stand on the promise, "Children are a gift from the Lord" (Psalm 127:3).

Periodically, we will invite anyone in our services who has been trying to have children to come for prayer. Anytime I go to another church connected with us, I always invite those people to come for prayer. An even greater thing, I always impart, (give away!) the anointing God has given us to that church and to anyone who wants to be able to pray over couples, many who've given up hope for having children. The gift He's given us can be experienced by everyone! When we pray over couples who have exhausted every medical resource possible to have children we have confidence the Lord will give them children! If you're reading this book wishing you could operate in the power to help couples have kids, ask for it. It's yours!

These are just a few of the hundreds of stories over the years of how God's faithfulness has been displayed in signs and wonders. It's important to note that there have also been times that our prayers and declarations for miracles haven't been answered like we thought they should have. That doesn't affect our resolve one bit to keep on contending for signs and wonders, knowing that God always does what's best even when we don't understand. He's good, and nothing can diminish that!

Let's join together and contend for the supernatural expression of signs and wonders. Paul says, "We are His workmanship, created in Christ Jesus for good works; which God prepared beforehand, that we should walk in them." We were made for this. If we'll do it, we can then, once and for all, remove it from the list of *The Best Kept Secrets In The Kingdom*.

The Mountains Are Talkin'!

.... and you've heard 'em too, whether you realize it or not! There's also a great possibility you've been listening way too much at what they're saying! I bet you're wondering just what I'm talking about. Well, Jesus knew we'd be facing mountains in the natural course of our life, so He addressed it upfront for us. "Whosoever shall say to the mountain, be removed and cast into the sea, and doesn't doubt in his heart that those things he says will be done, he shall have whatsoever he shall say."

Now, realistically I can't imagine why I'd ever want to move an actual mountain from one place to another. As far as I'm concerned, they're all exactly where they're supposed to be. On second thought, I wouldn't mind having a couple of small ones out here in Western Oklahoma just to look at now and then, but it is what it is. One would then have to surmise that maybe Jesus wasn't talking about a literal mountain at all but about the problems, obstacles, and potential dangers we all face in life.

I'd be surprised if anyone reading this little piece didn't have at least some obstacle facing them right now. It just seems to work out that way. Mountains talk a lot! And when you have one, the mountain will be in your face talkin' smack from the time you wake up 'til you go to sleep at night, sometimes even in your sleep! "You ain't gonna make it!". "You've got cancer!". "He doesn't love you anymore!". "Your friends are talking about you!". "You're a failure!". "You don't do enough good stuff for the Lord to love you!" The list goes on and on. Mountains are relentless! They don't let up! The more you listen, the more they talk!

I know you learned when you were a little kid to not "talk back." Talkin' back would get you in big trouble in those days. That was good advice then. But now, well now, things have changed. You gotta start talkin' back! I've found, for me, the most effective way to talk back to mountains is to find a scriptural promise that directly addresses the lies the mountain is saying to me. Every time that mountain tells me I ain't gonna make it. I'll declare the Word of the Lord out loud to my mountain. You can bet your boots I'm gonna talk back! And, I'm gonna do it like I mean it even if it feels like I'm spittin' in the wind.

That's exactly what Jesus did when He was tempted by the devil in the wilderness. Three times he appealed to logic in trying to deceive Jesus, each time Jesus answered with, "It is written....". Worked then for Him, and it'll work now for you if you'll just do it!

The payoff, you'll find that your level of faith rises every time you declare the Word to your mountain. Your mountain will begin to diminish in size. It's all about perspective. Your faith is being tested, and your faith will grow as a result.

So, yeah, the mountains are talking.

The question is, "What are you saying to your mountain?"

This and more thoughts from Andy can be found at his blog: "The Way I See It" - www.andyrtaylor.com.

PLAN OF ACTION:

- Awaken to the reality that signs and wonders ARE for today!
- Let the Lord nurture your appetite for signs and wonders
- Don't be discouraged if you pray for someone and it doesn't happen
- Ask the Lord to stretch your faith
- Ask for opportunities to pray for miracles

LEADERS:

- Develop a Scriptural basis for signs and wonders
- Teach your people
- Nurture their faith for miracles
- Believe for signs and wonders!
- Model how ministering for the miraculous should look

PRAY:

"Father, ignite my desire for signs and wonders. Thank You for opportunities to pray and declare for miracles to take place. Thank You for allowing me to participate in Your plans for the miraculous."

Spiritual Gifts

"Now concerning spiritual gifts, brethren,
I do not want you to be ignorant."
—Paul

The subject of spiritual gifts easily makes my list of *The Best Kept Secrets In The Kingdom*. I include spiritual gifts because of the position many in the church today have taken concerning the gifts in general. It's uncanny how Paul's statement, above, to the church in Corinth a couple of thousand years ago could still have as much relevance as it does for the church today. I would encourage anyone, individuals and churches alike, to take a serious look (or maybe, another look) at this important subject, get some help from the Holy Spirit and move into the operation and exercise of the gifts of the Spirit on a routine basis. The church has been thoroughly equipped by the Father to be a powerful organism to effect a Kingdom change in the earth. Without spiritual gifts, we're merely operating under our own steam.

When Paul said, "I don't want you to be ignorant …," he wasn't being critical or disrespectful. In fact, he was being very positive. He was saying that he did not want them to be uninformed or uneducated about spiritual gifts. Many today are uninformed, even more uneducated. There has been a lack of sound teaching on the gifts and in some cases the teaching has been downright bad. Those who have had no teaching whatsoever have a definite advantage over those who have had bad teaching. Because of that bad teaching many are convinced that the gifts are not for today. Or, because of manipulation and intimidation from some who try to force others to rise up to their own level of perceived superiority they've chosen to ignore the gifts, altogether. It's a subtle trick of the enemy to spread this kind of propaganda, and he's been very successful at it.

It's bad news for the kingdom of darkness any time a child of God discovers the authority and power that are available to them through the Holy Spirit. As long as one is marooned in a place of trying to operate under his own power, the Kingdom of God is void of the supernatural power God has destined. When that happens, it causes the church to be a benign, ineffective organization unable to transform society rather than being the dynamic organism with the power to change the world the Father has purposed it to be.

There are three main lists of gifts in the New Testament. (some would argue there are 4 or 5 lists and I would not disagree) The fivefold ministry gifts consisting of apostle, prophet, evangelist, pastor, and teacher are listed in Ephesians 4 (Further explained in chapter on Church Government). Another list is found in Romans 12:3-8. These seven gifts are commonly referred to as "motivational gifts" or "personality gifts," as I like to call them.

Romans 12:1-8 - Motivational Gifts - Personality Gifts

- **Prophecy** - Strongly opinionated, discerner, a realist
- **Serving** - Looks for ways to serve, practical, etc.
- **Teaching** - Systematic, Methodical, Love for the Word, Enjoys teaching
- **Exhortation** - Encourages, Positive, Visionary, Dreamer, Optimistic
- **Giving** - Liberal in giving materially, always looking for opportunities to give
- **Administration** - Organized, prioritized, stays on course
- **Mercy** - Compassion, empathy oriented, identifies with those hurting

The study on the motivational, or personality, gifts (Romans 12) is a real eye-opener in terms of understanding how the Father has blessed us in our personality. I've chosen not to include a broader study in this book, but I would wholeheartedly encourage everyone to do further study on them. The very best work I've seen to date is: *Discover Your God-Given Gifts* authored by Don and Katie Fortune. As you discover how He has gifted you, you'll begin to understand yourself and others in ways that could very well be revolutionary.

For the purpose of this chapter, I will focus on the list of gifts found in 1 Corinthians chapter 12, referred to as the "gifts of the Spirit." One of the keys to understanding the "gifts of the Spirit" is first to understand that "THE GIFT" is the Holy Spirit. If you've been born again, and the Spirit is now dwelling in you, the potential for all nine of the "manifestations" is resident in you right now and are available to you on an "as needed" basis!

Baptism in the Holy Spirit

John the Baptist made this statement in Matthew 3, "I indeed baptize you with water unto repentance, but He who is coming after me is mightier than I, whose sandals I am not worthy to carry. He will baptize you with the Holy Spirit and fire." After the death, burial, and resurrection of Jesus,

He spent time with His disciples. He said to them, "Receive the Holy Spirit," (John 20). In Acts 1, immediately before He ascends to the Father, Jesus says, "Wait for the Promise of the Father, which, you have heard from Me; for John truly baptized you with water, but you shall be baptized with the Holy Spirit not many days from now." In the same context, Jesus says, "But you shall receive power when the Holy Spirit has come upon you, and you shall be witnesses to Me in Jerusalem, and all Judea and Samaria, and to the end of the earth."

There were 120 people in that upper room. They were in "one accord," and of one mind. They were faithfully praying and waiting as Jesus had instructed them to do when all at once, they began to hear the sound of a "rushing mighty wind!" They visually witnessed what was described as "cloven tongues of fire" as the Holy Spirit fell on everyone in the room! They began to speak in "other tongues" as the Spirit gave them utterance.

This epic event took place during the Feast of Pentecost in Jerusalem. There were many different dialects present that day as Jews came from all the surrounding regions to observe the feast. Something utterly supernatural occurred as these faithful followers of Jesus spoke in other tongues; everyone there that day heard them speak in their own language. Truly amazing, to put it mildly! Peter stood up and began to speak about Jesus to the throng of people. When he finished, no less than 3,000 people were born again and baptized that day in Jerusalem. A day or two later, Peter and John approached the temple, and a man, lame from birth, was begging for alms. I would guess they had seen this man many times before but today something was profoundly different; Peter said to the lame beggar: "Silver and gold I do not have, but what I do have I give you: In the name of Jesus Christ of Nazareth, rise up and walk." Not only did the man get up, but he began leaping as he walked into the temple with Peter and John, praising God. You might even notice that they didn't even pray for the beggar. They just commanded him to rise up and walk. These two events are the first we see as a result of being "baptized" in the Holy Spirit. Jesus promised, "You shall receive power when the Holy Spirit has come upon you." The Greek word here for power is, "dunamis," where we get our English word, dynamite.

We receive the Holy Spirit when we're born again. However, baptism in the Holy Spirit is a separate baptism. It seems the simplest way to define Holy Spirit baptism is: "a supernatural empowering by the Holy Spirit for the work of the ministry."

There is much argument and contention over the initial evidence of the baptism of the Spirit. Many claim that the gift of tongues is always that evidence. There is a fair argument to support that since it was the evidence on the Day of Pentecost with the Jews and with Cornelius and his family, who were Gentiles. I choose not to engage in the argument but to say that the baptism in the Spirit is evidenced by power, and it could be evidenced by any of the nine manifestations listed below.

The question would arise as to how we can receive this baptism of power. It's as simple as just asking. For the life of me, I cannot comprehend anyone not wanting to operate under the anointing of the Holy Spirit and the power of God!

Gifts of the Spirit:

- **Word of Wisdom** - Insight into how given knowledge may best be applied to specific needs arising in the Body of Christ
- **Word of Knowledge** - The ability to discover, accumulate, analyze, and clarify information and ideas that are pertinent to the growth and well-being of the Body. Rightly applying wisdom
- **Faith** - To discern, and act with extraordinary confidence to the revealed will and purposes of God
- **Healing** - To cure illness and restore health apart from the use of natural means
- **Miracles** - To perform powerful acts that are perceived to have altered the ordinary course of nature.
- **Prophecy** - To receive and communicate an immediate message of God to His people through a divinely anointed utterance
- **Discerning of Spirits** - To know with assurance whether certain behavior purported to be of God is in reality divine, human or satanic.
- **Tongues** - (A) To speak to God in a language they have never learned and/or (B) to receive and communicate an immediate message of God to His people through a divinely anointed utterance in a language they have never learned
- **Interpretation of Tongues** - To make known in the vernacular the message of one who speaks in tongues.

There was a renewed emphasis on the gifts of the Spirit beginning with the Azusa Street Revival in Los Angeles in 1906. After that time, people began to seek the gifts, which in turn brought many reports of authentic, supernatural signs and wonders. Gifts of the Spirit caught much more momentum with the advent of the Charismatic Movement beginning around 1960. The movement began to lose momentum in the 80s and 90s and is not talked about much today. Many of the good characteristics have stood the test of time and today there are many individuals, ministries and churches faithfully contending for the miraculous. It's clear where that is happening, the Father is faithful to bring His power to set things in order according to His Kingdom purpose. Jesus' instructions on prayer included, "Let Your Kingdom come, Your will be done on earth, as it is in Heaven."

There is a swirl of controversy surrounding the gifts, more specifically the gifts of tongues and interpretation of tongues. Paul devoted more time in his teaching on those in his day because there was controversy even in the first century. There are theories today ranging from such extremes as, "Tongues are not for today and all speaking in tongues is of the devil," to still others who declare, "If you don't speak in tongues you're not saved." Both these are fundamentally incorrect, and the Truth is somewhere in between. It's our responsibility to search and seek out that Truth and not throw the baby out with the bathwater because of the controversy involved. This is a very important subject, so it's no wonder the enemy has tried to pervert the Truth. It is sad that he has been as successful as he has.

Summing up Paul's teaching on tongues leads to some obvious conclusions:

1. The gift of tongues IS for today and did not become obsolete after the Day of Pentecost, or after the demise of the first century Apostles. Paul's letter to the Corinthians was written 30 years after the outpouring of the Holy Spirit in Acts chapter 2.
2. The expression of tongues is useful for:
   - Prophecy, word of knowledge, word of wisdom or teaching in the corporate gathering (church service) provided an interpretation is given (1 Cor. 14:6; 14:13)
   - Praise (either corporate or personal) (I Cor. 14:15)
   - Prayer, commonly referred to as "praying in the Spirit" in a "prayer language" in an unknown tongue (either corporate or personal) (1 Cor. 14:15)
3. A message in tongues might be rare in the corporate gathering anytime there are those present who are uneducated, uninformed or are unfamiliar with the gift (1 Cor. 14:18-19, 23)

4. A form of the word, edify, is found no less than seven times in chapter 14! Tongues, as with any of the nine manifestations of the Holy Spirit, are to be exercised in an edifying manner undergirded with love and coupled with a desire to be a blessing to the whole Body. This brings life to the Body rather than dissent or confusion. It is obviously the "more excellent way" Paul is referring to in 1 Cor. 12:31.

If one looks closely at Paul's teaching and lets the Scriptures speak, it starts to become quite clear, and the controversies begin to dissipate.

I'm often asked, "Is it okay to seek after the gifts?" The answer is a resounding, "Yes"! When Paul says, "Desire earnestly the best gifts," he's actually saying, in the clearest interpretation of the Greek language, "to be zealously lustful for." So, you tell me, is it okay to seek after the gifts? There are others who say, "Well, we're to seek the 'Giver,' and not the gifts." More often when I hear that response it comes from someone who wants to deny the validity of the gifts for the church today. Of course, we're to seek the Giver. That's a no-brainer, but not at the expense of rejecting things the Giver wants to give us in the first place!!

Not growing up in church, I had absolutely no reference point for any of these things concerning the gifts of the Spirit. I did have what I call a "holy curiosity" for them when I began to hear and read about them. I recommend you have a holy curiosity, yourself. If you'll do that and pursue with a clean heart while searching for the Truth, the Father will show you, beyond the shadow of a doubt, these things are relevant, useful, and much needed in the church today.

We had only been going to church for a year or two when we were invited to go with a group to the James Robinson Conference in Dallas. In one of the services with 10,000 in attendance, and during a very quiet time during the worship, a man with a deep, booming voice stood up in the audience and gave a message in tongues. Even though it was my first experience (most of our entire group's first experience as well), it didn't blow me away; it didn't bother me. I was curious. When the eight couples of us got back to our hotel we were enjoying snacks in one room and talking over the service. One of my friends said, "What about that guy that gave the message in tongues?" I said, "Yeah, that was something, wasn't it? Julie, my wife said, "He wasn't speaking in tongues!" We jokingly argued back and forth a time or two but both holding to what we knew we had heard. Julie then said, "He wasn't speaking in tongues!" "Here's what he said." I don't recall what the message was but of the 16 of us in that hotel room exactly eight, some women some men, heard and understood exactly what the man said and the other eight didn't understand anything he said! That was proof to all of us that what happened was an authentic expression of the gift of tongues.

Another time I attended a revival meeting with a friend in what would be classified as a charismatic church. We sat near the back in the small, packed church with about 150 in attendance. The speaker invited anyone involved in worship to come to the front for a time of ministry. About 15 people went down. Soon, a woman on one side of the church gave a message in tongues. Again, I'm curious, somewhat fascinated, but not bothered in a negative way at all. I didn't understand anything the woman said. As she began giving the word in tongues the Scripture verse, "Out of the mouths of babes and infants, You have ordained praise", came to mind. No sooner did it come to my mind than a man on the opposite side of the church stood up and declared, "Out of the mouths of babes and infants, You have ordained praise"! I was such a novice at that point, but I believe the Lord had given me the interpretation of the message in tongues, as well, had I known to be obedient to step out by faith.

I tell these two actual stories to encourage you to have that "holy curiosity" I talked about and to pursue the gifts of tongues and their interpretation. The Father will take that curiosity and give you solid evidence for all the gifts. Some will cautiously stay away from the gifts because they may have seen or experienced others faking it. I don't like that either, but that's a bad excuse to not go after the gifts. Let's make a resolution right now to go after the gifts and to be genuine and authentic in our expression of them.

My goal here has not been to do an exhaustive study on the gifts, which could easily take an entire book, but to give you enough information to ignite your interest to the degree, you would start to investigate yourself. The most concentrated information on the gifts of the Spirit is found in 1 Corinthians 12, 13, and 14. In chapter 12 Paul lists the gifts and compares the Body of Christ to our physical body. In chapter 14, he writes as to how the gifts are to be exercised in the corporate gathering. Right square in the middle of those is chapter 13, commonly referred to as "The Love Chapter." There Paul conveys the absolute necessity of exercising the gifts in an atmosphere of agape, unconditional love. To do so otherwise is out of order and doesn't accomplish the Father's desired results. Paul concludes his teaching in chapter 14 by saying, "All things must be done decently and in order."

A Heart of Gold

Do you know anyone that you would describe as having a 'heart of gold'? You know, that person that possesses all the qualities you'd want to embrace yourself. I'd say a person with a heart of gold would be someone with integrity, someone who is always truthful, someone who is dependable, someone who is sincere, someone who cares, someone who has your back, someone who does the right thing, someone who is brave, someone who sees the best in everyone. You could take that list a lot further if you wanted to, but you get the point.

I think we're born with a pure and innocent demeanor, but it doesn't take long for the world, and all it throws at us to begin to tarnish those traits. The world is mean, indiscriminate, and it does its best to run over us. When it does, it just doesn't care. These things take a toll on even the strongest personalities. They can cause that pure and innocent demeanor, or heart, to be tainted. You know what they say, "The struggle is real!"

But there's good news; When we're born again, it's "Job #1" for the Holy Spirit to 'conform us into the image of Jesus'. Quite a task, if you think about it, even for Him. After years of learning to walk with the Lord, I'm more like Him than I was. But, in reality, I'm still a long way from being just like Him. The Father's plan to conform us into the image of His Son has nothing whatsoever to do with our appearance, as the bible verse might indicate. But it has everything to do with our heart being conformed to be like His!

Neil Young's song, "Heart of Gold," encourages the listener to "be a miner for a heart of gold." That's exactly what the Lord does when we come into relationship with Him. He "mines" those valuable qualities and traits that lie deep within our soul and brings them to the surface. We are, after all, created in the image of God!

I'm thinkin' we should do the same thing with the people we're in relationship with and the people we encounter. Maybe they're arrogant, disrespectful, and hard to deal with. What you see might not be 'who' they really are! Maybe they're just the result of the meanness of the world. But what if, deep down, everyone out there really does have a heart of gold that hasn't yet been "mined?"

Being that kind of miner starts with a determination to bring out the best in others no matter what it takes.

Let's you and me take the Father's example. Let's be "miners for a heart of gold!"

> *This and more thoughts from Andy can be found at his blog:*
> *"The Way I See It" - www.andyrtaylor.com.*

PLAN OF ACTION:

- Investigate the Biblical basis for the gifts of the Spirit
- Allow Biblical Truth to challenge faulty systems of belief
- Make a strong resolve to "walk in" the Truth you learn
- Ask to be "baptized" in the Holy Spirit
- Start immediately relying on the Holy Spirit for His power in your daily life
- Commit to being an edifying factor in your church

LEADERS:

- Learn about the gifts of the Spirit and begin to teach them
- Take your time to help your people understand
- Let your people see you "walking" in the gifts
- Teach on the gifts and let your people see you "model" how they should be exercised in the corporate gathering
- Continue to reinforce the necessity of the gifts
- Testify, and communicate the supernatural results as you see them

PRAY:

"Father, I desire to learn about spiritual gifts.
I desire for all the gifts to be functional in my life to the degree
You desire. Holy Spirit, I trust You to use me as You see fit,
and to the fullest extent of the Father's will."

Moving in the Prophetic

"A prophetic word in season has the powerful potential to adjust and set someone's life on course."
—AT

It seemed necessary to include a separate chapter on the prophetic because of its importance in the scheme of spiritual gifts, and the fact Paul talked about the gift of prophecy more than the other gifts listed. Because of things discussed in the previous chapter and the reality that prophecy is so seldom used, and used in an edifying way in the church today, it is definitely to be included in *The Best Kept Secrets In The Kingdom*. For the purposes of this chapter, my definition of prophecy is the ability to speak forth a message from God, which is received from the Holy Spirit as it is brought forth.

"But earnestly desire the best gifts. And yet I show you a more excellent way." Paul then launched into one of the most beautiful pieces of literature ever penned writing about love. That's the "more excellent way!" He's not talking about a casual, skin-deep kind of love but agape, unconditional love. The highest quality of love the Father loves with. God doesn't just have love; He is love! He concludes 1 Cor. 13 by encouraging the readers to, "Pursue love, and desire spiritual gifts, but especially that you may prophesy." "For he who speaks in a tongue does not speak to men but to God, for no one understands him; however, in the spirit, he speaks mysteries. But he who prophesies speaks edification and exhortation and comfort to men. He who speaks in a tongue edifies himself, but he who prophesies edifies the church. I wish you all spoke with tongues, but even more that you prophesied; for he who prophesies is greater than he who speaks with tongues, unless indeed he interprets, that the church may receive edification."

Prophecy is a very important gift as it edifies the church. It's a very powerful gift indicated by Paul's admonition to desire the "best gift." Notice he says, "one who speaks in a tongue edifies himself." Paul isn't saying tongues is not important today, as some people argue. In fact, he says that it has an edifying effect on those who exercise the gifts. I think that's important. If we are to be an edifying factor in the corporate gathering, and to the whole Body, it makes sense that we do what we can to be edified, ourselves.

Old Testament Prophecy vs. New Testament Prophecy

In the Old Testament, prophets were mostly men handpicked by God and filled with His Spirit to: Lead His people, warn of impending danger, strategy to defeat enemies, encourage His people to turn from sin, and many other things. One of the key distinctions between Old and New Covenant prophets is in the Old Testament days the prophets were nearly always speaking to people who did NOT have the Holy Spirit. But Joel prophesied, "In that day I will pour out My Spirit on all flesh; Your sons and your daughters shall prophesy, Your old men shall dream dreams, your young men shall see visions. And also on My menservants and on My maidservants I will pour out My Spirit in those days." Since the Day of Pentecost, and the outpouring of the Holy Spirit, we are living in that time. Now, those who prophesy may, or may not, be speaking to people who have His Spirit. Big difference. The biggest difference is that now, we may all prophesy! I have observed that there are very few who actually operate in the gift of prophecy. I think that is a serious problem. Some of the contributing factors why more don't operate in prophecy include: Some have never been taught. Some err in believing prophecy ceased with the Old Testament prophets while others just believe it isn't needed today. Those reasons, and more, are a poor excuse for not acknowledging, learning about and acting on prophecy today. Individuals as well as the entire church would be much more effective if we would decide to move into the gift of prophecy. An even greater problem I see for those who haven't totally rejected the idea of spiritual gifts, and prophecy in particular is the fear of missing and subsequently being labeled a "false prophet." Let's unpack that theory.

Dispelling the Fear of Being Labeled a "False Prophet"

There is a common mindset, even among those who believe the gifts are relevant for today that anytime you give a prophecy that doesn't come to pass, it falls under the category of false prophecy. Not true! False prophets in the Old Testament prophesied in the name of false gods, such as Baal. So, don't buy into that lie.

Any person can look at their own life and see things they're good at. Maybe they are good pilots, golfers, or counselors. Any one of them will tell you that on their way to being proficient in whatever the discipline might be, they made many mistakes along that path. Learning from those mistakes made them much better at their craft. Much better, in fact, than if they'd never made a mistake to begin with. It seems that in the church people are afraid to "step out" in prophecy afraid they'll make a mistake. The result is a church that believes in the gifts but never exercises the faith it takes to operate in them. For people to become comfortable using the gift of prophecy (as with the other gifts) there must be an environment that gives them room to "fail." It may sound dangerous but it's not. In fact, it's very healthy for individuals and the church. As a leader I recommend we encourage our people to step out by faith. Of course there needs to be sound teaching as well as demonstrating how prophecy should be used. When those factors are in place it serves as a "safety net" and people will begin to properly exercise the gift of prophecy. Now, if someone consistently "misses" with their personal prophecies we may have to pull the person to the side and give what I call, "soft correction." The last thing I want to do is to discourage the person. I'll encourage them by commending them for stepping out in prophecy. Then, I'll instruct them in ways that will help them in the future by being more edifying to individuals, and to the Body. If we expect our people to operate in the prophetic we must do everything we can to simplify it for them and to help them mature in the gift. When Paul says, "For you may all prophesy," he's saying, "You can do this stuff"! I believe it's what the church needs to hear today.

Prophetic Stories

Julie and I were eating in a restaurant in Oklahoma City while on a Christmas shopping trip. A middle-aged couple and a young man in his early 20s, which I assumed was their son, came in and sat one table away from us. The Lord immediately drew my attention to the young man. I casually observed them, glancing periodically and being careful not to let them notice I was looking their way. I had nothing, just the strong feeling that there was something spiritual that needed to happen. We finished our meal, paid our ticket, got in our car and left the restaurant. Almost immediately, as we drove away, I said to Julie, "I think I missed the Lord." I explained how the trio had captivated my attention, and I was sure it was the Lord. She hadn't even seen them as they were seated directly behind her. I said, "I've gotta go back." The street we were on was undergoing construction, so there were no opportunities to turn around for a couple of miles. It took the better part of ten minutes. Finally, I got my chance to turn around and drove straight back to the restaurant. (Just so you can see that I'm far from perfect in this I must confess that in the back of my mind

I was kind of hoping they would already be gone.) They were still there. I approached their table. I still had NOTHING! Just the strong feeling the Lord had something important to say to the young man, who I was sure was their son. I said, "Excuse me." "Sorry to interrupt, but I think the Lord has something He wants me to tell y'all." "Is that OK?" They said, "Yes. Sure" The moment they agreed, the Lord gave me the word for the young man. (Actually for the trio, as they were his parents). "The Lord says the way you make decisions is like a "gunslinger." You shoot first and ask questions later. You're a very quick decision-maker. God has made you like that and He loves that about you!" By this time all three are nodding their heads in agreement. "You have a big decision in front of you that He doesn't want you to make in that way." "It's a very serious decision." "God wants you to make it, only after you've diligently prayed about it." "God will let you know exactly what you should do." That was it. I asked, "Does that make any sense to you?" They all nodded in agreement as the mom said, "Oh, yes!" "We know exactly what that is!" I asked if I could pray with them, to which they agreed. I did so and went on my way. We made our way to the mall, Julie went in to shop, and I stayed in the car. I can't explain why I began to weep deeply. I can only guess the decision facing the young man was extremely important, and that God wanted him to "slow up" so he could receive His counsel on it. To this day, when I tell the story, I'm still brought to tears. I always think of how close I came to missing God's appointment with them.

The fact he was a quick decision-maker is not necessarily prophetic. Often the Father will give you a personal characteristic (something you would have no way of knowing) about the person, as He did in this instance, to help validate the word that's about to be delivered.

As I was greeting people after a Sunday service 15 years ago, a couple who I had met but didn't know well, came by. As I was greeting them I had the feeling the Lord had a word for them. (Again, I had nothing!) I asked if I could pray with them and they agreed. As I prayed I had a vision of them being involved in foreign missions. I asked, "Has the Lord said anything to you about serving in foreign missions?" In unison they laughed and said, "No!" I didn't let it bother me. I thought, "Well, I missed the Lord on that." I had missed before. The couple were not regular attenders and they lived an hour away. I think it was the last time I saw them. I did see a mutual friend a year or two later and asked them about the couple. The friend said, "I haven't seen them in a while." "They're in Uganda on the mission field." You can imagine my astonishment!

About ten of us from our church were planning a trip to Florida to a ranch on Lake Okeechobee with about 100 men who were there working and going through a very successful, Christ-centered, drug treatment program. There would be another 50 or so men such as us from churches around the U.S. there to connect with one another, and to learn from noted speakers, Bob Mumford, Dudley Hall, Doug White, and Jack Taylor. A week before we were to leave the Lord said to me, in that still, small voice, "While you're there I want you to deliver a message to Jeff." I had absolutely no idea who Jeff was. I prayed every day the Lord would give me the message He wanted delivered to him. Nothing! I was to speak at the night service with all in attendance, both ranch hands and ministry people. During the invitation I said, "The Lord has told me that I'm to give a message to Jeff." "So, Jeff, if you're here, I'd like to pray for you." Soon a young man came down and said, "I'm Jeff." I prayed for Jeff but got absolutely nothing from the Lord in the way of prophecy. In a few more minutes a couple of the staff from the ranch brought another young man. His name was Jeff Sayre. (My church is in Sayre, Oklahoma. Nearly always when I'd seen someone with that last name it had always been spelled, Sayer, not Sayre!) I thought to myself, "This is the Jeff I'm looking for!"

I prayed for Jeff. NOTHING! Absolutely nothing prophetic for this Jeff, either. I thought, "Well, I must've missed the Lord on that!" I was somewhat bothered since I was sure the Lord wanted me to give a prophetic word to Jeff. The next day in our ministry meetings (ranch hands not present) a young man who was present in the day meetings the day before, whom I had seen but not met, approached me. "Hey, I heard you had a word for someone named Jeff?" "I wasn't at the service last night, but my name's Jeff." "I'm from Nashville." "Would you pray for me?" As soon as I touched this young man the Lord gave me a very clear vision! I saw the downtown streets of a large city but there was no one on the streets. They were totally desolate. There was a strange feel about the city. About two blocks down on the right, and around the corner of a skyscraper, I saw what I knew to be horses with glowing red eyes snorting fire and smoke, being ridden by demonic-looking figures. I couldn't tell how many but there appeared to be five or six but I somehow knew there were many more.

As I prayed for Jeff the Lord gave me the word. "Jeff, the work you're doing in Nashville is extremely significant." "You're going to be very successful." "There is a demonic troop seeking to trap and snare you with PRIDE. They're watching and waiting for an opportunity to attack you and the work God has before you." "You're to draw even closer to God, grow deeper in relationship with Him, be accountable to your other leaders and keep an eye yourself not to let pride find its way into your life." It was a sobering prophecy and one that Jeff took to heart. Obviously, I finally found the right, Jeff!

I could tell dozens of more stories like these of how God has used me to deliver a prophetic word. I've missed Him plenty of times, and I don't like that feeling. I'd rather miss trying to do the right thing than to play it safe for the rest of my life. I think the Lord likes that! If you'll ask the Father to use you in delivering personal prophecies, He will use you, as well.

The "Acid Test"

Old Testament prophecy was sometimes harsh and judgment-oriented with an ultimatum attached and, in some cases, final. New Testament prophecy differs in that, as Paul so clearly writes, the prophetic word must be one of edification, exhortation, and comfort. "But he who prophesies speaks edification and exhortation and comfort to men." In 1 Corinthians 14 a form of the word, edify, is found no less than seven times! He further clarifies, "Even so you, since you are zealous for spiritual gifts, let it be for the edification of the church that you seek to excel." Prophecy that fits the criteria and given in a loving way has the potential to edify and bring life to the entire Body, as well as any individuals who might receive the prophetic word. I have been asked more than a few times a question such as this; "I had a dream about a close friends' daughter." "She was in a very bad car wreck." "Should I tell my friend?" Well, based on our established criteria, "No!" It's not edifying, not encouraging, and not comforting. In fact, it's exactly the opposite of those. In that case, we should pray. God will often give you something of this nature that isn't meant to be a prophecy given, but a "heads up" to pray about the situation. When the Father finds you faithful in the things He gives you, He will share many things like this with you.

Practical Application - Fleshing it Out

Receiving the Prophetic Word: If you're going to be available to the Father to be used in the prophetic start now to prepare your heart. I've said that receiving the prophetic word from the Lord is the easy thing. The harder thing is to know what to do with it. Should I give the word now? Later? Not at all? These are questions you should ask of the Lord. At any rate, the first thing we should do when we think we're receiving something prophetic is to pray. Ask the Lord for direction. He will let you know His will. There will be times that the word is crystal clear. There are other times, like the stories in this chapter, you may feel you have nothing. You know the Lord has something for that person. In those cases, you'll learn to step out and give your prophetic word. (taking into consideration the other factors in this chapter). Sometimes the Lord will be clear and specific; other times, He can be just as vague. It takes more faith to prophesy when He's vague, but when He does that, He's pulling you into a deeper level of faith. It takes more faith to give a word that's not extremely clear. He knows you have adequate faith to do it, and He'll do this to prove to you that you have it too!

Very often, the prophetic word you give someone serves to confirm things the Lord has already been showing that person. The fact you had absolutely no knowledge of that is a powerful thing to that person and has a way of shifting them toward God's plans for their life. It proves, beyond the shadow of a doubt, that what they've been hearing (and wondering about) is from the Lord.

A Prophetic Word:
- Restores value
- Provides direction
- Enhances vision
- Unlocks secrets in a person's heart
- Activates your destiny!
- Provides insight in personal ministry
- Can break bondage/curses
- Increases faith
- Vital in spiritual warfare!
- Serves to grow the faith of the giver and the receiver
- Revelation of God's will
- May confirm things God has been saying to you
- God's way of adjusting, accelerating our course (Destiny)

Personal Prophecy

Very often, the word you receive from the Lord will be a personal word for someone. In that case it's not something that the whole Body needs to hear. As you grow in the prophetic you'll be able to discern if it's personal or something that should be delivered to the Body. There's a thing I call "prophetic etiquette." I may have a very clear word for someone, but I'll usually ask, "I think I have a word for you. Is it OK for me to give it to you?" I hardly ever give someone a word without asking for their permission. (unless it's for someone close to me that I'm around all the time) If the person says, "No", then I'm at total peace to not give them the word. For those willing to be used by the Lord in prophecy, it's wise to develop this prophetic etiquette, and we need to learn to be OK if they're not in a place to receive.

Prophecy in the Corporate Gathering

Sometimes the prophetic word is one that has the potential to bless the entire Body. It's important to understand authority as well as the protocol that your church may have adapted for prophecy. In our church, not just anyone can come and get the mic and give a word. There are those, however, who are seasoned and have proven themselves in similar situations that can be trusted, and that happens fairly often. Daryle Perry has a strong prophetic gift. I can read him like a book when the prophetic spirit is on him. I may even ask him, "Do you have a word?" When he does, it's always relevant, always timely, and always edifying. For others believing they have a word for the Body, I'll have them give the word to Daryle or one of our elders and let them decide if the word should be given to the whole church. If the elder(s) agree it should be given, we then allow them to deliver the word. This is a safeguard to ensure the word that is given doesn't cause confusion or division. As leaders, it's our responsibility to protect our people. This prophetic protocol has worked well for us. I recommend every church develop their own system of procedure for the prophetic so it will be edifying, and life-giving.

Giving a Word of Personal Prophecy

- Don't ever be forceful!
- Ask them if it's OK for you to give them a word
- You're not responsible for what the person does with the word
- I always ask them to "test" the word
- What happens if you miss?
- Don't beat yourself up
- Learn from it and prepare to be used again
- You'll be "sharpening" up your prophetic edge
- Don't try to make the word make sense to you! (It's not for you!)

Practical Tips:
- Has He "given" you something?
- Is there a "prophetic" feel?
- Has He drawn your attention to someone?
- When someone else is praying, is God showing you something?
- Do not speak out of the flesh!
- This is not your opportunity to tell the person what you think they need to do!
- God often gives "symbolic" words or pictures

Positioning Yourself to Hear From the Lord
- Deal with personal unbelief
- Prepare your heart
- Agree with God's will
- Grow in your intimacy with the Father
- "You have not because you ask not"

Obstacles to Moving in the Prophetic
- Unbelief
- Religious orientation
- "Not for today"
- Bible Belt mentality—"That's for the ministry people."
- Fear
- Lack of confidence
- Afraid you'll "miss"
- Fear of being labeled "false prophet"

Judging a Prophetic Word Given to You
- Each of us is responsible to examine and judge personal words of prophecy given to us
- Be careful who prophesies to you!
- Does it edify, comfort, encourage?
- What is the "spirit" behind the prophecy?
- Does it contradict Scripture?
- If so, it must be judged as inaccurate!
- Does it glorify, bring honor to Jesus?
- Is it relevant for you?
- Does it confirm something that the Lord has been speaking to your spirit?

- Is it manipulative, critical, or controlling?
- Is there condemnation attached?
- These are warning signs. Pay attention!

Are You Ready?

- Accept the Truth of Scripture
- Give the Holy Spirit permission to use you
- Listen, ask, pursue!
- Resolve to be obedient
- Use your faith
- Stop worrying that you'll miss!
- Enjoy the adventure!

A Prophetic Dream and a Defining Moment

God has a broad variety of ways He can speak to us. If you think about it and understand that He's a Father, you'll understand that He always wants to communicate with us. It really comes down to us tuning into His frequency, if you will, and receiving by faith what we hear. God is not limited to speaking to us in an audible voice. I know plenty of people who say they've heard Him that way, and I believe them. But the Bible lists numerous other ways He speaks to us, and some of those include dreams and visions.

I can't say I've had a lot of prophetic dreams; maybe a few dozen, in the years I've been learning to walk with the Lord. But the ones I have had were very profound and life-altering, to say the least. One such instance happened nearly 32 years ago. We had moved off the ranch in the Texas Panhandle and were just a month or two deep in starting the church. In the dream, it was if I was in a classroom with about 15 people in it. They were all sitting in those desks like you used in high school. All of these people were reaching out for me and moaning and groaning in a very defeated and agonizing tone as if to be crying out for help.

On top of that, they were all covered with some kind of bluish, green substance. One of the women toward the front of the classroom reached out for me, but as she did, her arm just broke off and crumbled like a piece of brittle pottery. Another man got up and started toward me, but as he stood, his leg broke like the woman's arm, and he fell to the floor. I walked up to another person, still in his chair, to pray for him, and I put my hands on his head. When I did, I noticed that the bluish-green substance (the best description I can give is that this substance had the texture of that blue cue stick chalk used to play pool, but it was also damp) had a terrible smell to it. The smell was so bad that it was making me sick to my stomach. I should insert here that nothing makes me sick enough to throw up. Only done that a few times in my whole life. My family knows if I start throwing up, they better call the undertaker! (LOL) In my dream, the smell was making me sick enough to throw up. It was at this point I woke up. I sat up in bed as quickly as I possibly could and actually gagged for about 30 seconds. I didn't throw up, but I came as close as you can without doing it. That was the end of the dream.

At that precise time, I had no idea what the dream might mean, but the next morning the Lord began to give me some specific insight into what it meant. He showed me the brittleness of the people in the dream represented what dead religion does to a person. It makes us rigid and fragile. (as opposed to supple (teachable) and strong) The hopeless nature of the people in the dream was a result of what religion does to us, without the life-giving component of our relationship with the Father. The blue-green substance was also the residue of religious mindsets that smother the life out of us. I believe the sickening smell I experienced is exactly what the Lord experiences when we are bound up by lifeless religious thoughts and practices but have no relationship with Him!

The Lord spoke very clear to my spirit in His still, small voice; "Andy, My people, are smothering and dying because of dead religion. I'm sending you to deliver my people from that bondage and to set them free."

That's been years ago but still very fresh in my mind. Looking back, it now seems crystal clear to me that it's what my life is supposed to be about. That dream has served to form me and shape me into 'who' the Lord wants me to be, ...and 'what' He wants me to do. And, looking forward, I believe I can trust Him to continue to carry out that mission through me and the people He's assembled here if we'll simply keep on being obedient to Him.

This and more thoughts from Andy can be found at his blog:
"The Way I See It" - www.andyrtaylor.com.

PLAN OF ACTION:

- Use your faith to overcome your fear of operating in the prophetic
- Learn to listen to the Lord
- Ask for the Holy Spirit's help
- Ask the Lord if He has a word for someone
- Be obedient to what you hear
- You'll miss much less than you think!

LEADERS:

- Cultivate an atmosphere conducive for the exercise of all the gifts
- Your people will not move in the prophetic if you don't
- Teach and model the correct ways of delivering prophecy
- Apply soft correction when someone misses or delivers awkwardly
- Develop prophetic protocol in your church

PRAY:

"Father, I desire to operate in the prophetic. Help me to be sensitive to Your Spirit at all times. I want to be someone You can trust to be obedient to Your words. I desire to exercise my faith anytime You want to use me in this way."

Church Government

"For this reason I left you in Crete, that you should set in order the things that are lacking, and appoint elders in every city as I commanded you ...."
—Paul

How is the church to be governed? That's a very good question and one I think should be answered immediately, considering the opportunities that exist for the Body of Christ in the world today. There are plenty of models out there and certainly no lack of opinions, but only a Biblical model will suffice. It obviously belongs among *The Best Kept Secrets In The Kingdom* because of those many opinions. The challenge here is to address such a seriously vital question in limited space and time.

I'll state upfront that there is certainly no criticism nor condemnation toward anyone, leaders, or otherwise, who might find themselves outside what I will present here. It can be a controversial subject but, obviously, God can do whatever He pleases and He's famous for blessing anything that has His Name on it. Let's agree on the premise that we all want not just a partial blessing on what we're doing in terms of ministry, but the full blessing of God.

I think it's safe to say that most today would lean toward the idea of the church operating as a democracy. A model where everyone has a voice and, in most cases, likewise has a vote. While that may work perfectly in some secular environments it doesn't appear to be a Biblical model. One great example is when the spies went into the Promised Land. Keep in mind that the Lord, Himself directed that venture. It's important to note that He did not send them there to decide whether or not to go, because He had already given them the Land. I would simply call it a mission of reconnaissance, to see what they were up against.

You know the story; one representative of each of the 12 tribes was chosen. I would guess that these were proven men; men who were sensible, mature and not given to careless or rash decisions. After they returned this was their report. Ten of the men said it was, indeed, a land flowing with milk and honey, BUT there were giants inhabiting the land. Joshua and Caleb had an entirely different report. They, too saw the giants and said they were so big and intimidating they made them feel like mere grasshoppers. BUT God had given them the land! That's when they had that famous "business meeting" and voted 10-2 to stay out of the Promised Land. Long story, short; because of God's anger at their disobedience every living person over the age of 20 (except Joshua and Caleb!) died there in the wilderness over the next 40 years. To sum it up, ten men, who incidentally died right there on the spot, kept 3-4 million people out of the Promised Land. There are several lessons in this story, but one glaringly obvious one is that those who follow unrighteous leadership are subject to the same penalty as the leaders themselves. We're responsible to discern the hearts and motives of our leaders. To summarize: A democratic form of church government where a board hires and fires pastors while demanding he do "only" what the board dictates is not a Biblical one.

Another model, although not as common, is the autocratic rule or what I call the "one man show." You'll find this most often in smaller churches. With this type of church government the leader has unlimited or uncontrolled authority. What he says goes! He may even have a board he calls elders or deacons. They're not there to participate in the decision making process but only to agree with the "man" to help him enforce his own personal agenda. In John's short letter, (3 John 9-12) he talks about a man with this form of leadership. "I wrote to the church, but Diotrephes, who loves to have the preeminence among them, does not receive us. Therefore, if I come, I will call to mind his needs, which he does, prating against us with malicious words. And not content with that, he himself does not receive the brethren, and forbids those who wish to, putting them out of the church." This man was intolerant of the ministry of the apostles who had been sent by God. This is a dangerous scenario for numerous reasons, not the least of which is a total absence of accountability. This type of leader routinely makes unilateral decisions wanting no one else's opinions and expects everyone to comply, or else.

Even another common model of church government is one where a "board" rules. It could be called an elder board or even a deacon board. Some might even call it a board of trustees. *(not a Biblical term, by the way) Sure sounds safer than the previous example, and probably is. If this board takes the reins of the church and controls the man of God by demanding he does only what they tell him to do, it's, again, a form of church government that is out of order, based on Scriptural evidence. A true leader who has a correct heart and God-given vision is hardly ever allowed the liberty to implement the things God wants to do unless it fits the board's criteria. You'll find this form of church government often, and in those churches where it's the norm, it's not rare to see several pastors come and go in a short time. A true leader who understands the call of God on his life can't thrive in this scenario. The church will always be what it has always been. At the same time, there may be positive things happen in the church. As I stated before, God will bless, to some degree, anything professing His Name. This form of church government may also move forward by a vote of the people. The board makes recommendations, and people are free to decide and to vote their conscience about important matters. There is more accountability in this model, which is a plus, but it's still not the best-case scenario.

There are yet other churches that are under the rule of a central organization. The sister churches may operate under the same by-laws, hold to the exact same statement of faith, and some even preach from the same Biblical text every Sunday. This model is less common, but it does exist.

There are some profound church government principles found in Acts chapter 6. Let me frame it up: The new church in Jerusalem was thriving; people were being gloriously saved and baptized and learning to find their place. A problem arose when the Hellenistic Jewish widows were getting short-changed at the daily food distribution. Something had to be done. "The apostles summoned the multitude of disciples and said, "It is not desirable that we should leave the word of God and serve tables." "Therefore, brethren, seek out from among you seven men of good reputation, full of the Holy Spirit and wisdom, whom we may appoint over this business; but we will give ourselves continually to prayer and the ministry of the Word."

Here, you see the distinction made between elders (or bishops) and deacons. The apostles, who are also elders in this story, weren't saying they were too good or too important to serve food to the widows. Although in our current church culture, they would surely be accused of such. No, much to the contrary, these men knew their "call" and knew they must devote themselves to prayer and the ministry of the Word. It's all a matter of function. Elders are the decision making, direction dictating body while deacons (and deaconesses) carry out the day-to-day service tending to the natural needs of the church, such as the above example. Elders are no more important to the Body of Christ than are the deacons. It takes both! One possible difference is that the office of an elder is a God-ordained office while deacons may be appointed. Doing so, however, without prayer and serious deliberation, would surely open the door for error. So, it appears the early church was governed through the faithful activity of elders and deacons working in conjunction and harmony with one another.

When the church was born in Jerusalem on the Day of Pentecost, the growth was phenomenal. The church exploded, literally overnight! The Kingdom of God was being advanced and gaining momentum by the day. The Holy Spirit was having His way in the hearts and lives of the people of God. It was truly unlike anything the world had ever seen before. So, the ministry of the apostles (elders) and deacons was vital to the health and well-being of this "new" thing called the church. Both those groups were learning to function in their calling. The church during that time was doing so good the Lord added to it daily, those that should be saved.

Soon we see the apostles and prophets working together.

Acts 11:27: "And in these days prophets came from Jerusalem to Antioch." Then we see the emergence of teachers.

Acts 13:1: "Now in the church that was at Antioch there were certain prophets and teachers."

Acts 21:8: Luke referred to Philip, who incidentally was one of the seven men chosen to serve as a deacon, as an evangelist. Paul concentrated his teaching on those ministries to the church in Ephesus, adding the office of "pastor" bringing the total to five.

Eph. 4:11-16: "And He Himself gave some to be apostles, some prophets, some evangelists, and some pastors and teachers, for the equipping of the saints for the work of ministry, for the edifying of the Body of Christ, till we all come to the unity of the faith …."

These five gifts are commonly referred to as the fivefold ministry. It's important to note that these are not titles, as is common in church culture today, but job descriptions.

In modern religion, the fivefold ministries have been virtually ignored by much of the Body of Christ. While most religious groups acknowledge the ministry of pastor, evangelist, and teacher, the ministries of apostle and prophet, are almost universally rejected. Many would argue they're not for today. Interesting, when you consider the Bible clearly states in Ephesians 2:20, the ministry of apostle and prophet are the "foundation" of the church. Could the omission of these two vital ministries be one of the key reasons the church in our generation is weak and ineffective? When the foundation of any structure is faulty, the entire building is shaky, and its integrity is compromised, to put it mildly.

I propose we take another look at the fivefold ministries, pray and lean on the Lord to see their emergence in our generation today. The future and destiny of the church, I believe, depends on it. While entire books could be written about this subject, I'll give brief descriptions of these five gifts of people (both men and women) to the church.

Apostle - An apostle is simply, "one who is sent forth." When asked, "How many apostles in the Bible?" most would answer, "Twelve." We're familiar with Paul, who most would consider to be the most prominent Scriptural example, but not one of the original twelve. Would you be surprised to know that there were as many as ten or more listed besides those? Apostles receive their call from God, Himself. They're sent forth as ambassadors of the Kingdom of God. Included in the gift mix of an apostle is the keen ability to set things in order in the church. They have an eye for what needs to be adjusted and a supernatural anointing to identify those who God has His hand on as elders. Paul recognized and ordained leaders in all the cities and regions where he ministered.

Most people think Paul was a church planter, but in reality, his gift was more directed to bring healthy organization to the believers (the church) that were already in those cities. The influence of an apostle enables the church to keep moving and to not "set up camp," so to speak, where the church can become stalled out, inwardly focused, and unproductive.

Prophet - The office of prophet is a uniquely fascinating call on a person and extremely valuable to the life of the church. While the Bible states, "we may all prophesy," the mantle of a fivefold prophet has a much broader scope. The prophet's anointing enables him to see "down the road," helping the church to build according to the instructions and pattern the Lord has given. The prophet, both foretells (about things to come in the future), and forth-tells (speaking things presently relevant). This helps us to understand why apostles and prophets worked so closely together in the Bible in the building and advancement of the church and the Kingdom of God. These two, working in conjunction with one another, add a synergistic component and brings powerful results to the church.

Evangelist - "One who announces good news." While we should all be purveyors of the good news the fivefold anointing of evangelist enables this person to not only tell the good news but do it in such a way as to cause the hearers to desire to make a heart decision to follow Jesus. Philip was led by the Spirit from Jerusalem to the Gaza desert, where he encountered an Ethiopian eunuch. This person served closely with Candace, the Queen of Ethiopia. Philip told the eunuch the good news of Jesus. He received Philip's words, was born again, baptized, and went on his way home. Historians tell of the eunuch's arrival in Ethiopia, where he, likewise, told the good news to his people. The result was a great awakening where thousands upon thousands were born again into the Kingdom. So, as you can see, the evangelist has the supernatural ability to present the good news in ways that causes others to make a decision to follow Jesus and to train others to do it as well.

Pastor - "Shepherd; one who tends a flock." It's interesting that our current church culture has made an institution of the ministry of pastor. Most would be totally surprised to find out that the word is used only one time in the entire New Testament. While the fivefold office of pastor is valid and needed for today, it would serve us well to take a closer look at the Biblical definition. The Greek word, *poimen*, simply means shepherd. These days the person with the title, pastor, is expected to be good at everything from preaching and teaching to counseling, visitation, conflict resolution, expert on finances, and an unseen list of about 4,000 other things, some Biblical and valid, others obviously not. It is the title given to the head of the church in our culture. I love to give my best example of what I'd call a fivefold pastor.

Early in my walk with the Lord in my little church in the Texas Panhandle, there was a man by the name of Lee Hall. Lee had the uncanny ability to know how everyone in church was doing. He knew if they were or weren't doing well spiritually. He knew if they'd lost their job or if they had a sick child. He knew if they had a need of any kind, and he was quick to help to meet the need, whatever it might be. A perfect example of a shepherd. He wasn't the leader or point man of the church. Lee never preached a message that I know of. In fact, if you were to tell him he was up next Sunday to preach, he probably wouldn't even show up. He had no title, but no one knew the state of the flock or took care of them like he did. Our religious tradition has skewed the ministry of the pastor, and we some times have expectations of the person given the title to the degree that it's extremely unfair. A fivefold pastor might very well be the point man of the church, but there's not one thing in the Bible that says the point man might not have an apostolic anointing, the anointing of a prophet, teacher or evangelist. When we try to force someone into a man-made organizational structure, we might very well be forcing them into a spot they're in no way equipped for.

Teacher - Simplest definition of the five; a teacher is one who teaches or instructs. A fivefold teacher has a supernatural anointing to research, organize, and present Biblical truths in a way that people can understand and adhere to. The teacher is very methodical in the way he presents the message. His anointing enables him to "ground" those under his teaching in the Word and to help them mature in the things of the Lord. It's of utmost importance to the teacher that those hearing his message would be able to understand and then walk in the truths he presents.

How the Fivefold Ministries Can Work in Conjunction with the Local Church

One of the best Biblical examples of how the apostolic and fivefold ministries works is found in Exodus 18. Moses was God's man to lead His people out of bondage in Egypt, no question about it. His father-in-law, Jethro (a type of apostle), went to the camp of the Israelites to check on his daughter and her family. He saw Moses standing all day long listening to the problems of the people and immediately said to Moses. "This thing you're doing is not good. It's not good for you, and it's not good for the people." One can easily see why it would not be a wise thing for Moses. If all you're getting done is listening to the problems of the people from daylight to dark day in and day out you're probably not getting much "leading" done. While the people's problems are very important there are other people who can do these things. It's even been proven and well-documented by those who are willing to depart from the traditional "pastor does everything" model that many of these "other" people can do some of these things much better than the pastor. What's more important, this frees up the "man of God" to actually lead the flock.

Jethro counseled Moses to do something totally different. Remember now, Moses was God's man. Whatever he decided to do with his father-in-laws advice was his call. Jethro didn't have to answer to God for the leading of the Israelites; Moses did. Moses did heed the word of Jethro and chose 70 men to do what he had been doing. They handled all the problems of the people, but if they ran into something they couldn't handle, they brought the issue to Moses. It says later on in the book of Exodus that God put the same spirit that was on Moses, on the 70. It worked exceptionally well then, and it'll work exceptionally well now. It could take time to get smooth at it, but in the final analysis, everybody wins!

The thing to see here in terms of how the apostolic works is, let's say someone with an apostolic anointing is brought into a local church. The man of God for that situation is the pastor, or "point man." The apostle has a supernatural anointing to see things that need to be adjusted like Jethro did. He may give the pastor and leadership of the church any number of things they could do to enhance the effectiveness of the church. Just like with Moses, it's the pastor and his leadership team of elders that are responsible for the final decision if they should do those things or not. Any mature apostle would not go as far as to force the church to adhere to their advice. The outside ministry (apostle, or anyone who holds a fivefold office) only has as much authority as the local leadership gives them.

Spheres of Authority

Any of the fivefold ministries may be present in the local church. There are others who may have a broader sphere of authority. We would call that having a trans-local anointing (being identified with more than one location). Some may have a regional ministry, while others may even have an anointing over an entire nation. Local churches may develop a relationship with any of these fivefold ministries and look to them for wisdom, advice, accountability, and oversight. This is Biblical and can often give churches profound, and much welcomed momentum. There is a Biblical provision as to how these fivefold ministries may be compensated (See page 160, paragraph 4 in this book).

Fleshing it Out

Best case scenario is that every church would have all five of these ministries among their flock and learning to function there to bring spiritual health to the entire Body. In the real world, it's hardly ever the case, although it is definitely something to work toward. In the meantime the Lord will use whoever he has and that person might function in any of the five gifts until others are either raised up, or brought in from the outside. The bottom line is: The fivefold ministries bring the life of God and balance to the Body of Christ. They have the anointing to cause the church to be what she's really supposed to be. It's only my opinion, but there is plenty of Biblical evidence to back it up, but without apostolic influence, every church is in danger of reaching a plateau and "settling in" and thereby taking on a maintenance mentality where it can become stagnant and ineffective.

Qualifications of Elders or Bishops

1 Timothy 3:1-7 - "This is a faithful saying: If a man desires the position of a bishop, he desires a good work. A bishop then must be blameless, the husband of one wife, temperate, sober-minded, of good behavior, hospitable, able to teach; not given to wine, not violent, not greedy for money, but gentle, not quarrelsome, not covetous; one who rules his own house well, having his children in submission with all reverence (for if a man does not know how to rule his own house, how will he take care of the church of God?); not a novice, lest being puffed up with pride he fall into the same condemnation as the devil. Moreover he must have a good testimony among those who are outside, lest he fall into reproach and the snare of the devil."

Qualifications of Deacons

I Timothy 3:8-13 - "Likewise deacons must be reverent, not double-tongued, not given to much wine, not greedy for money, holding the mystery of the faith with a pure conscience. But let these also first be tested; then let them serve as deacons, being found blameless. Likewise, their wives must be reverent, not slanderers, temperate, faithful in all things. Let deacons be the husbands of one wife, ruling their children and their own houses well. For those who have served well as deacons obtain for themselves a good standing and great boldness in the faith which is in Christ Jesus."

Obviously there is a high standard set for leadership, as it very well should be. However, in the modern church, those having experienced divorce have been disqualified from being elders or deacons or having any leadership position, whatsoever. While that is unfortunate and definitely not to be preferred, it should not be the "death penalty" for those who have recovered, have proven themselves faithful, and now walk in obedience to the Lord. In Bible times, it wasn't rare for a man to have more than one wife.

Unless Paul had a wife we don't know about, he was not in compliance with the strictest interpretation on the qualification of "must be the husband of one wife," himself. This can be a very controversial matter, especially in a denominational environment. One should consider Moses, who killed a man; David, who had a man killed; and Paul, a zealous instigator for Christians being stoned to death. All three went on to have great influence for God and the establishment of His Kingdom. It seems divorce should not disqualify someone today. At any rate, those being considered for any leadership position should be carefully observed, and their character thoroughly scrutinized by other leaders to safeguard and minimize further problems.

Summary

The fivefold ministry of apostle, prophet, evangelist, pastor, and teacher are given to the Body of Christ to edify and equip the saints for the work of the ministry. For the church to come into its fullness, these ministries must be understood and brought into full view. Fivefold ministries may be present in the local church or brought in from the outside to work with the pastor, elders, and leadership team. The model we see in the New Testament is that of a "plurality" of God ordained elders with the point man or pastor being the "lead elder." This Biblical model eliminates the danger of a "one-man-rule" and places the many important leadership responsibilities facing every church squarely upon the group of elders. We have been operating under this model for over 30 years, and it works extremely well. Our elders (six besides me) understand that I have the vision for the "house," and there might be a time where that would be the difference maker in an important decision. In 30 years, I can't think of a single time that we weren't in full agreement on an important issue before we moved forward. This is a very Biblical, and therefore safe, method for leading the church. Rather than limit what the church can accomplish, it frees up a strong visionary leader and enhances the church's potential to fulfill its God-given vision.

Some churches may choose to designate a board such as a board of trustees. While this isn't a Biblical term, I see no harm as long as the determination is made by the existing leaders to appoint such a board. Sometimes an advisory board can be very helpful on issues such as finances. The key is to educate the board as to their responsibilities and limitations, or by default, they will think they're to "run" the church. I have seen some real problems occur where an advisory board decided to become a governing board. Clear communication at the outset is the remedy.

I'm often asked, "Will God bless our church if we're not doing this in an exact manner?" My answer is, "Yes," but with a disclaimer. "Do you want the full blessing of God or just a measure of His blessing?" The answer seems quite clear but one of the obvious roadblocks is that hardly anyone has seen this type of church government, which leads them to think it must be wrong. It's important to note that if a church wants to move to a more Biblical model of government, a few things must be considered. Any change must be done in compliance with the current by-laws and change must be clearly communicated and done slowly but deliberately, understanding that tradition always dies screaming! We have helped a number of churches make this transition. It's never easy but well worth the effort.

We have entered a "season" where God is blessing the church in a myriad of ways, especially where there is a resolve to do things His way. This type of church government would be called a theocratic model, or better put, God's rule through His appointed men and women. As you can see, it's no mystery why church government is on the list of *The Best Kept Secrets In The Kingdom*.

Theorists and Practitioners

Theorist: *Someone who considers given facts and comes up with a possible explanation is called a theorist.*

Practitioner: *Someone who is actively involved in real-life situations and qualified to practice a particular occupation, profession, or religion.*

I had a conversation ten years ago with a few close friends. I don't actually remember the exact details of the entire conversation, but I definitely remember the conclusion I came to soon after it was over. I was with four other ministry people, all of which had quite a few years of experience. A couple of these guys are great communicators, orators, Bible teachers. But they weren't actively involved in the day to day dealing with people and their problems. It's not that they couldn't do it; they have. It's just that they weren't heavily involved at that time. I'll call them the "theorists." They're important people; they're good at what they do!

It was a really good, brisk discussion on how things ought to work in the church from a strictly Biblical standpoint. On those topics, there wasn't much disagreement whatsoever. But the 'rub' came when we began talking about how it really is in the "trenches." You know, out there where the rubber hits the road in real life; Where you get knocked down, get your nose bloodied, betrayed, lied to, lied about, tripped up and derailed. That all can happen (and really a lot more!) in the process of 'practicing' the theory, especially in ministry.

I am deeply involved in the day to day challenge of dealing with people and their issues. I' been doing it for over 30 years. It's what I do. I'm far from perfect at it, but I have learned a few things. For that reason, I'd say I'm more a 'practitioner' than a theorist. When you add, what I'd call the 'human factor', to any theory, even a Biblical one, it complicates that theory to a large degree. Doesn't mean the theory is wrong or even faulty, for that matter. But it's different when it's being lived out in real life. It's never quite as neat; in fact, it's usually pretty messy; it's never as cut and dried as we'd like for it to be. When you add people to the equation, it gets a lot more difficult. It's nearly always worth it but difficult, nonetheless.

It led me to this conclusion; There needs to be a 'coming together' of the 'theorists' and the 'practitioners'. They need to sit down at the table and talk, discuss, compare, hash it out, even argue a little if it's friendly and helpful. It's vital, I think. If it's done in a productive manner, everyone leaves the table wiser and better equipped, and both have a much better understanding.

In all truth, and I think this is how the Lord designed it for obvious reasons, unless the theory is tested in the laboratory of life, all you have is a theory. But when the theory is a Biblical one, and the parties involved will lean toward the Lord, it usually works out a whole lot more often than not!

The theorists and the practitioners need to get together!

Readin' a book about learning how to fly an airplane is fine, but when you're taxiing down the runway, things get REAL!

This and more thoughts from Andy can be found at his blog:
"The Way I See It" - www.andyrtaylor.com.

PLAN OF ACTION:

- Execute your own due diligence on Biblical church government
- A great resource: *The Church in the New Testament* by Kevin Conner
- Maintain a resolve to move to a Biblical model

LEADERS:

- You're responsible to teach elders and deacons their responsibilities
- Unlike a secular organization such as IBM or Apple, where the CEO rules from the top down, the church is different. Leaders rule in the Body of Christ from the bottom up with the heart of servants
- You're not looking for "yes" men but those whose hearts are "given" to God and have no personal agenda
- Clearly and consistently communicate any changes that need to be made
- Your church needs to know that "where" they are going is better than where they are
- Move slowly but deliberately
- Stay the course!

PRAY:

"Father, help me to understand and function in Your pattern for church government."

Toward More Powerful Prayer

"God does nothing except in response to believing prayer."
—John Wesley

Unless I miss my guess, you're surprised that prayer is included among *The Best Kept Secrets In The Kingdom*. Just so you don't forego reading this chapter because of it, I'll say upfront, "You're going to find some things in this chapter that you probably haven't thought about, and definitely some things that will help you have a victorious life, ministry or church!" Having said that, it's normal for everyone in the church to already know that prayer is important. What I've found in assisting other churches and ministries is, even though everyone knows its important, very few churches give prayer the value it deserves.

Prayer is one of the greatest privileges we've been given by the Father. It's His preferred way for us to communicate with Him. For believers, it's not *if* we pray, it's *when* we pray. Prayer should be one of those things that we give the highest priority. It should be something we're not willing to neglect.

I spent a few days with a couple from another state recently. They drove the 5 hours here to meet with me for marriage counseling. At the end of our counseling sessions, I began to instruct them about how they should pray. This couple has been faithful to attend their church for a number of years. As I explained just the basic tenets of prayer I could tell that they'd never heard the things I was saying. I asked them a few simple questions about prayer, and if they'd had some teaching, but they answered, "No." I'm afraid it's not an isolated incident. That tells me that not every church approaches prayer with the greatest importance. Is it possible that prayerlessness is one of the great deficits of the modern church? I've found that to be the case more often than I'd like to admit. It would certainly explain why the church is not making inroads into our culture the way it should. The good news is it's an easy fix if one's willing to make the commitment. For individuals and churches who do, the results could be dramatically transformational.

I have also noticed that many church growth conferences, that are loaded with good speakers, tips, and resources, often omit any prayer instruction. In my mind, and in my experience, prayer should hold a place of preeminence in the life of any church. When I started attending church in tiny Allison, Texas, in 1985, one of the first things I noticed was a strong commitment to prayer by my pastor, Ronnie Chadwick. It was about the time that Dr. Cho's church in Seoul, South Korea (One of the largest churches in the world; over 800,000 members) was making the headlines. Dr. Cho was a strong proponent of prayer. At that time he was consistently teaching on prayer; corporate prayer (praying together with others in small or large groups) was a high priority; in addition to that Prayer Mountain was established to provide a secluded place of prayer for those who desire a place to be alone with God and to engage in a period of extended prayer. Larry Lea, at that time leader of the fastest growing church in America, Church on the Rock in Rockwall, Texas, had made a trip to Korea and caught the importance of prayer and began to implement it in his Texas church. He did a great teaching series on prayer titled, "Could You Not Tarry One Hour?" using the Lord's Prayer as a model. Our church went through the entire series, and we began to implement a strong prayer ministry as well. We prayed every weekday morning from six am to seven am and ten until Noon on Saturdays. The results were phenomenal! Our church began to grow at an alarming rate. People were driving an hour or more to this little, out of the way town to experience the moving of the Lord. Dozens were getting saved. People were acknowledging the call of God on their lives for ministry. That's been over 30 years ago now, and there are at least eight couples who are still serving the Lord in full-time ministry. Keep in mind that this little town only had a grocery store, post office, and a livestock feed store. That just says that wherever God finds a people who are willing to seek Him first and make a commitment to pray and do what He says, He will defy all odds to bless them in ways that can't be explained any other way.

    Those early years were life-altering for me. It built in me a good foundation and a strong commitment to prayer, both individually and corporately. From the start in Sayre, we implemented a mid-week prayer time. Wednesday mornings at 7:00 am, people would gather to bring their petitions to God. The group was small at first but grew over time. When we started to experience phenomenal growth in the mid 90s I told the congregation, "If you wonder why you're seeing the amazing things you're seeing, you should come to our Wednesday morning prayer time. These are things we've been praying for!" Even today, the importance and necessity of prayer is still a constant and indelible facet of our spiritual DNA.

Personal Prayer - Corporate Prayer - Intercessory Prayer

Personal Prayer

It's self-explanatory. I don't think it should take a lot of space to define. What I do think is important is for each individual to consider making personal prayer a predominant part of their overall spiritual life. The benefits will present themselves immediately upon doing it. It's important to remember that prayer, in its simplest form, is communication with the Father. All productive communication is two-sided; talking and listening. So, it makes sense that part of our prayer time should be offering our needs to the Lord. It's equally important to listen to the Lord as well. I've found that if I listen, it shortens my list of things I need to ask of the Lord. I'm often asked if it's selfish for a person to pray for themselves. Absolutely not! In fact, it's mandatory! Of course you should pray for yourself. It's important to voice those things to the Lord that are on your heart. Some believe it helps to set aside a specific time for personal prayer; others just do it at any random time or as a need arises. I was recently surprised in my own church when I asked for a show of hands of those who were struggling in their prayer life. The number was at least 75%! I was shocked and immediately scheduled a message on prayer to boost the personal prayer life of our family. At any rate, make it a priority, find whatever works for you, pray in specifics and be consistent. Nike's tagline fits well in the prayer scenario: "Just Do It!"

Corporate Prayer

Corporate prayer is the term used to describe praying together with other people—in small or large groups. It was an important part of the church, and in Acts 2:42, we learn that the early church prayed together: "They devoted themselves to the apostles' teaching and to fellowship, to the breaking of bread and to prayer." For us, our personal prayer time differs from corporate prayer in that when we come together to pray, it's for more than just personal needs and concerns. This is when we pray for the larger scope of our church. Listed below are some of the things we regularly include during our corporate prayer time.

- All areas of ministry in our church
- The vision of the House
- Prayer for the property (100 acres on Interstate-40)

- National & State leaders: The President, his Cabinet; Congress; Our state Governor, etc.
- Praying over our city and the surrounding region. (Trinity is more than a "local" church. I'd describe it as a regional church.)
- City Leaders: City Mgr, Mayor, Council; School Board; Court House
- We pray for the churches and ministries connected with us
- We pray for the Lord to add to that number
- We call in the harvest from the North, South, East, and West
- We engage in a time of spiritual warfare as the Spirit directs
- We pray for the other churches and ministries in our city and area

This is not a conclusive list but one that will give you some idea of what we do to help you as you initiate corporate prayer with your people or in your church.

During our corporate prayer time some years back, I felt the Lord directing me to start praying over Interstate 40. We're 26 miles from the Texas state line; our church property is only a couple hundred yards from the highway. He directed us to pray for anointing and protection over local law enforcement as well as Oklahoma Highway Patrol and the Drug Task Force. We prayed that there would be huge number of drug busts made on the stretch of highway from the state line to the neighboring town to the East, Elk City. We did that faithfully for several years. An Oklahoma State Trooper and his family started going to church with us and he came to prayer one Wednesday morning. He heard us pray, as we had been doing, over I-40 and the drug traffic. He stayed after prayer and asked me, "Do you have any idea what you're praying?" I replied, "What do you mean?" He continued, "Do you know that the number one drug interdiction agent in the United States works this area you're praying for?" He definitely had my attention! "He said, "There are more drug busts made in this area you're praying for than on any stretch of highway in America!" He began to tell us story after story of the drug busts made, many within just a few miles from where we're located. There are many very miraculous stories that I don't have space for here, but it made us believe that because we were obedient to what we heard the Lord say, and stayed consistent in praying those things, we were able to play a strategic role in stopping at least some of the drug trafficking across America. Incidentally, in the 15 years that we've been praying this I've seen no less than five drug busts out my office window that faces I-40! We have declared this to be a "Kingdom Zone!" That's just one story; there are many more. We've had people to stop in and say they have no idea why they got off the interstate, but that the Lord directed them here. We've even had a few that drove up, came in, and without any explanation, say, "I need Jesus!" Those kind of happenings can only be the direct work of the Lord. When a commitment is made to pray, you can count on God doing miraculous things!

When we come together for corporate prayer there are things we are aware of that need to be prayed about. We also understand there are things that we don't even know about yet, but the Holy Spirit does. We acknowledge that and try to be sensitive to the Spirit as He breathes those things into our spirit.

Intercessory Prayer

Andrew Murray, the great South African writer, teacher, and pastor, said of intercessory prayer; "We know too little of persevering, persistent prayer, and that is indeed one of the greatest needs of the church." Of course, we're all called to pray, but there are those in every group that would say that their main ministry is that of prayer. We call these people intercessors. An intercessor is one who "stands in the gap," or intercedes in behalf of others. We intentionally identify those in our church who fall into this category. A time of training is necessary, and as leaders, we monitor their activity to help them mature in their calling. Intercessors are a very valuable asset to any church. As they prove themselves faithful, discreet, and trustworthy, we may begin to give them critical and sometimes sensitive issues to pray for. As you might assume, confidentiality must be a very important factor of the intercessor's ministry. As a leader, I'd advise keeping clear and consistent communication with all intercessors. This can be a powerful ministry if initiated, maintained, and overseen by seasoned leaders.

Prayer Projects

Over the years, there have been a number of special prayer projects we felt prompted by the Lord to conduct. One such project happened as a result of a vision the Lord gave me during our Wednesday corporate prayer time, not just once but three weeks in a row. The city of Sayre had gone through all the due diligence actions, and the decision was made to build a private prison here. It would be the largest prison in the state at the time. Not knowing the will of the Lord about the prison, we had prayed from the first talk about it three or four years before. Construction took a few years.

Fast forward to the completion of the prison. Construction was completed, but there were breakdowns in contract negotiations for a couple of months. Even though there was a full team of employees (200-300), there were still no inmates in the facility. Three weeks in a row, the Lord gave me a vision of myself and a team of people going into the prison to pray throughout the entire facility. The third week immediately after prayer a woman, who I had seen in church but didn't know, had asked one of the staff leaders at the prison call me. She was having a bad day and asked if someone could come to the prison to pray for her. By now, the recurring vision was much more than mere coincidence in my mind. I drove into the parking lot of the prison. I prayed, "Lord, if this is You wanting us to pray over this prison, You'll have to put me in the company of the people who can make that decision." I went through the second door into the prison and came face to face with the Warden, Assistant Warden, and the Chief of Security, the three top officers of the prison. I said, "The Lord has given me a vision of us bringing a team of people inside the prison and pray over every square inch of the facility." I continued, "That's probably against every rule you have, but if you would allow us to do that, we would bring in a team to do it." When I left the prison that day, I didn't have much confidence it would happen. In fact, I thought I had probably scared the prison leaders so badly by the story of the visions that they wouldn't want anything to do with it. Amazingly enough, they called the next morning and said, "We want it to happen!" We planned the project for the next week. We fasted that day, and about 20 of us met at the church at 5:00 pm, prayed for an hour, then drove the few miles to the prison and entered there at 6:00 pm. We broke up into three groups, prayed through the offices, the cafeteria, and every single cell in every single pod. One of the guards who was put in charge of leading us through the facility opened up to the group he was with. He had been involved in a shooting incident in another prison some years before that resulted in the death of an inmate. He couldn't forgive himself. The group prayed for him, and he then confessed he needed Jesus. They prayed with him right then and there to be saved! It took about three hours to finish the project. The three teams ended up in a large room with an optimistic feeling of completion. We ended with praying that whatever the holdup with negotiations would be solved within a week. It was! Within a week, plans were made to start sending inmates to the prison. We have maintained a presence there for the past 20 years, holding weekly services with many inmates saved and set free!

Another interesting project was initiated when we asked if we would be able to pray through the Beckham County Court House. Again, we thought it would probably be prohibited. Not so! We were given the keys to the Court House! A team of 15 of us went in after hours and prayed over the entire building, all the county offices, judges quarters, and the courtrooms. An amazing thing happened when we finished the project. We exited the Court House, and there in the sky was a perfect cross, directly over the city of Sayre formed by two different vapor trails. Maybe it was the Lord's way of saying, "Job well done!"

More recently, I felt I heard the Lord tell me to walk every street in our town and pray over every street, every business, every house, and even every vacant lot. As I walk I pray and declare, "Lord, let the people who live here step into their God-given destiny." "Let Your Kingdom come on every block and in every business in town."

Other projects included praying through the newly completed County Jail, City Hall, the School Administration Building, and the entire school facilities, including cafeterias, gyms, and athletic fields.

These examples will give you some idea of what the Lord might want to do with you and your church. The key is to listen for His voice and be sensitive to what you believe He's saying to you.

The church in our generation should be full of life. It should be influencing every neighborhood in a loving way. It should be replacing pockets of darkness with the Light of the Lord Jesus Christ. The life, success, and results (or the lack thereof) of every church is directly connected to the level of its commitment to prayer.

It shouldn't be, but a deep commitment to prayer is one of *The Best Kept Secrets In The Kingdom*!

Prayer Changes Things

It was the message on a little plaster of Paris wall hanging at my Grandmother's house in Wheeler, Texas. (My Mom's Mom) I never knew my Granddad; he was killed in a motorcycle accident earlier in the year that I was born. That left her to raise three kids who were still at home. (2 older ones already married) She was an incredible person, in my opinion, and I've grown to appreciate that more and more as I've gotten older and understanding more of what it takes to raise a family.

One of my favorite things to do was stay overnight or a few days at her house. I still vividly remember bedtime at her house. There were two beds in her room...one for her and one for Herman, my uncle, her youngest son. (only three years older than me) There'd be a story or two before we all fell asleep, and they were always good ones. *(Herman always tried to tell a scary one, so we'd sleep with a butcher knife under our pillow for safety! lol) One story she told me when I was three or four years old was of an 'old, old Grandmother by the name of "Mamaw Teak." Well, that name 'stuck' and I called her that for the rest of my life.

When you're a single mother with three kids in a small town, you just have to do what you have to do to make ends meet. I remember her working at cafes and cleaning houses for people. Coming home completely worn out, but cooking one of the best meals that you could possibly imagine. One of my most memorable Christmases was when Herman, my brother Monty, and I got our "Rifleman" rifles. We maintained a high level of justice on that block and kept the bad guys at bay in Wheeler, Texas, for a good long while!

I think, somehow, the importance of prayer was imparted to me back in those days. That's one of the things we'd do every night that I was at her house. Looking back and assessing her situation, I think she lived by it! They lived a simple life, a good life, but a simple life. They got by on the provision of the Lord.

There's a lot more to say on the subject of prayer. But simply put, "Prayer Changes Things!"

This and more thoughts from Andy can be found at his blog: "The Way I See It" - www.andyrtaylor.com.

PLAN OF ACTION:

- Develop and nurture a personal prayer habit
- Be faithful to pray
- Pray in specifics
- Ask the Holy Spirit for help
- Be consistent
- Consider keeping a prayer journal to chronicle thoughts/insights

LEADERS:

- Make a deeper prayer commitment for your church/ministry
- Train your people in the basics of personal prayer
- Arrange a time for corporate prayer

- Listen to specifics of how/what the Lord wants you to pray
- Be consistent even if you're the only one praying
- Tell of the things you see the Lord do as a result of prayer
- Identify those called to intercessory prayer and train them
- Listen/look for opportunities for special prayer projects
- Consider appointing someone to head-up the prayer ministry

PRAY:

*"Father, teach me to be a prayer.
Help me so that my prayers are powerful."*

RESOURCES:

- *Taking Our Cities for God* by John Dawson
- *Could You Not Tarry One Hour?* by Larry Lea
- *This Present Darkness* by Frank Peretti
- *The Joy of Intercession* by Joy Dawson
- There is an unlimited number of good prayer resources to sharpen up your personal, corporate or intercessory prayer life.

The Pursuit of True Worship

> "The hour is coming, and now is, when the true worshipers will worship the Father in spirit and truth; for the Father is seeking such to worship Him. God is Spirit, and those who worship Him must worship in spirit and truth." (John 4:23-24).
> —Jesus

Worship of the Father is arguably the greatest privilege we have in our lifetime and maybe even in the age to come. I do know we will be worshiping throughout eternity. We won't be able to help it! As we grow in relationship with Him, true worship is a natural response to "Who" God is. You may wonder why it's listed in *The Best Kept Secrets In The Kingdom*. Worship, in itself, is not a secret. The priority placed on it, or the lack thereof, easily earns true worship its right to be included.

Just about anything we do and do with the right heart could be classified as worship. For the purposes of this chapter, I'll limit my comments to those times we participate (hopefully) during our church services as we sing praises unto the Lord.

The Importance of Worship

> "If we don't understand worship, how can we teach people about it? And, if we don't teach people about it, how can we expect them to participate in it? And, if people don't engage in worship, how can we expect to invite God's presence in our churches (services)? And, if we don't invite God's presence in our churches, how can we expect His power to operate in people's lives? And, if His power is not operating in people's lives, how can we expect anything other than a lifeless church. And, if all we have is a lifeless church, how can we expect to change the world?"
> —Zach Neese, *How To Worship a King*

The year was 1985. Soon after my life made the dramatic turn in 1984, I made a trip to Pampa, Texas, sixty miles away on business. Living in a "dry county" Pampa was the nearest place we could buy beer. I didn't go there often but when I did go I made sure not to leave town until I picked up a case or two of beer. You know, for medicinal purposes. LOL On this particular trip I did the usual purchase and headed home. I drank a few beers, maybe six, on the trip home. Let's just say I was feeling pretty good. That week there was a revival being held at the Baptist Church.

The speaker was a close friend of my uncle, Jack. I was feeling so good I thought, "Heck, I'll just go to church tonight!" So, I did! The place was packed; 150 people or more were packed in the small building. I found my place on the very last row at the back. I knew most of the people there, and I couldn't miss the look of astonishment on their faces when they saw me come in. Soon the pastor gave a short welcome, and someone I didn't know stepped up, had everyone stand up, and I knew we were about to sing some songs. Well, this was much different than what I expected. I figured we'd sing a few hymns from the book in the little holder on the back of the pews. No! They had a video screen with someone placing transparencies with words to these songs on them.

Little did I know that this little Baptist church had only recently introduced some praise choruses. There were some "catchy" little tunes, but I wasn't about to join in! That was totally off the map for what a Baptist church might do, especially in those days in the Bible Belt! Almost instantly, many of the people started clapping their hands and singing; some even raising their hands. I knew these people. They were normal folks, not given to fanaticism at all. Now, keep in mind, by this time in my life, I might've been in a church only a dozen times or less.

I had no idea what anyone did in church, but I knew this was wrong! Only the "holy rollers" did stuff like that! I couldn't believe what I was seeing. This was going way too far! I decided to ride it out. I made up my mind that as soon as that last, "amen" was said, I was heading for the door. I did exactly that. To my amazement, and I don't know how he did it; (must've been supernatural!), the speaker beat me to the door. Truth be known, I think Jack probably gave him a "heads up" to watch for me in the rare possibility I might actually show up for a service. He greeted me, said a few words, and I made my escape. I knew he could tell I'd been drinking, but he didn't let on like it.

That was really my first experience with church. It was for sure my first experience with any kind of singing like that. I was sure I didn't want to have to experience that again. Sometime in the months that followed, God started dealing with us about going to church there. As you might guess, I was very reluctant at the start. It turned out to be one of the wisest decisions I've ever made. Not only did we start to go regularly, but it wasn't long before we were singing those little praise choruses along with everyone else, and clapping too, if you can believe that!

The following testimony from a leader in one of our connected churches captures how special worship is to the Father, and just how serious He is about it:

> My pastor was a great man of God. I learned so much from him, and his influence in my life runs very deep. Here was a man who, at that time, had been a Southern Baptist pastor for 30 years. He had caught the importance of worship and was making great strides leading the church to a deeper level of intimacy and worship. He was totally going against the grain of what every other Baptist leader was doing. Naturally, he became a target for their jokes and criticism. But, it didn't phase him. Something happened during that time that I'll never forget. In many rural communities, the churches are small, and just about every church has what I'd call a "church boss." He's usually one that has some strong financial stability. That person has usually outlasted several pastors, and more often than not, things are going to be done his way, no matter what. Well, there was such a person fitting that description in our church. He didn't like the fact that we had moved away from the Baptist Hymnals, and he was going to do something about it. He had enough influence with some of the people that he could usually get his way, even if it took a while to get it done. He'd made the statement more than a few times that he wasn't having this 'praise thing' going on in "his" church. His manipulation of the few he could persuade was beginning to be very noticeable. Long story short, right in the middle of that, he had a debilitating stroke that nearly took his life. This person was never a factor in any decision the church made again. I learned there, at that point, just how serious the Father is about worship.

Where a commitment toward worship has been made God will do anything to protect and nurture it. It was there in that little Southern Baptist Church in Allison, Texas, that I became a worshiper. We had some glorious times there. The Lord met with us during our times of worship. Amazing things happened because a commitment was made to worship the Lord, no matter what!

When we started in Sayre, one of the first things I heard from the Lord was, "If you'll be obedient to Me in worship, I will lead you into new avenues." I had already been somewhat exposed to worship in our church in Allison, Texas, but I had absolutely no idea what the Lord might have been talking about at that point. I also remember the Lord saying that He wanted our church to lead our region in worship. At the time, a person was leading the singing. I wouldn't call what he was doing worship at all. In fact, it was about as far from true worship as you could get. I took this person to a few worship conferences so he could get a taste of something genuine, but he just couldn't get it. He would scold the folks in our little group and shame them into raising their hands or clapping. It was as bad as you could imagine. I had several heart-to-heart visits with this person in an attempt to help him catch the revelation of worship, but it didn't happen. It ended after church one Sunday when he called me a false teacher, got in his car, peeled out, and slung dirt and gravel on me. The commitment to worship remained.

One of the older ladies in our small little group had the bright idea that we needed to equip the kids with some rhythm instruments. Mistake!! The next Sunday, a little four-year-old sitting directly behind me had something that made an irritating "clacking" noise. He never stopped throughout the entire song service. Never in time with the songs; clack, clack, clack!! You can't imagine how bad it was for me. I made a vow if I somehow made it through this service that "clacker" would never be seen again. Miraculously, I did make it through the service, and the clacker was mysteriously gone forever. Our little building was just a quarter-mile from the North Fork of the Red River. You can use your imagination as to what might have happened with the infamous, little "clacker!" I have a dozen "nightmare" stories I could tell of our experiences in pursuit of true worship. Looking back, it was all worth it. The Lord had imparted a deep hunger in me for worship. That hunger still remains today.

What is Worship

We actually worship for one basic reason: God is worthy of our worship! He deserves it! While there may be a myriad of definitions of worship, I can simplify all of them by just one little sentence; Worship is an accurate response to Who God Is! It really is that simple. Our worship to God is payback to Him for all He's done for us. As we deepen in our relationship with Him our worship naturally deepens, as well.

> God's love is perfect, but it's not perfected until we choose to love Him back. Worship is our way of telling God, "I love You!"
> —AT

I've learned so much from my kids about my relationship with the Father, but this one is priceless. Saying," I love you" has been a regular, consistent, and heartfelt thing around our house since Julie and I were married 43 years ago, and it still is today. We were only married a year when Clint was born and our lives have been rich, as parents of 5 phenomenal kids. I've found that God is faithful to instruct us in whatever situations we find ourselves in. But being a parent offers, maybe, the best scenario of being in the "school of life" and for learning from Him.

When one of my little boys (I'll withhold his name so as not to risk any chance of embarrassment) was just beginning to learn to talk, I'd catch myself 10-15 times a day telling him "I love you," to which he'd reply, "I yub oo too, Daddy." First off, I do love him, but the Lord got me to thinking about it. It became apparent that the thing that I enjoyed the most about it was that I loved to hear him tell me in his unique little way that he loved me too.

The Lord showed me that my little boy had absolutely no idea whatsoever what the word "love" meant. And for you and me and our understanding of love compared with God's concept of love is exactly the same. Although we're learning, there's still a great distance between our understanding of love and what love means to Him! He doesn't just "have" love; He is love!!

Here's what I learned:

1. When you tell someone that you love them, it means to them what love means to them!
2. So when my little toddler said, "I yub oo too, Daddy," it meant to me what love means to me! That's why I loved hearing it as much as I did. We have a need to be loved, and hearing it is important.
3. So, (It gets better!) when you tell the Father that you love Him; it means to Him what love means to Him!
4. So, as our understanding of love grows, and even if there's a vast difference in our understanding and His, keep telling the Father you love Him because He really likes to hear it!!

"Who" is God to you?

"Knowing" Who you are worshiping profoundly affects how, and how deep your worship will be. If you only know God because of how someone else has described Him, your worship will be distant, also. If you fear Him, you'll worship Him out of that fear. If you think He's let you down, your worship won't be wholehearted. This may be offensive to some, but if you only know Him based on what you've read in the Bible, that's great, but it's an incomplete image you have of Him. We must taste and see, through relationship and interaction, that God is good! When we begin to see and relate to Him as Father, everything changes! When you do that, worship just happens!

"You can only love God to the degree you understand His love for you."
—AT

Benefits of Worship

The benefits, or rewards, that exist for us as true worshipers are many, but worship for the sole benefit of receiving those benefits is misguided, indeed. Worship is FOR God! If we're doing it for any other reason, or for what we can get out of it, it's contaminated. It's not true worship. Listed below is an abbreviated list of the benefits of true worship:

- First in order of importance - Brings honor to God
- When we draw near to God, He draws near to us!
- Gets your focus off you - Destroys selfishness
- Prepares, and calibrates your heart
- Tills the ground in our heart, so the Word takes root!
- Sets your heart in order - It serves to re-set our hearts
- Causes faith to rise up
- Where all kinds of things happen!!
- People are set free
- Addictions are broken
- Lives are put back together
- People are physically/mentally/emotionally healed!
- His Spirit of reconciliation invades hearts
- Relationships are healed
- Puts all your problems in perspective
- Drives heaviness away - "Put on the garment of praise" - Is 61:3
- Scatters the enemy
- Corporately = Tangibility of His presence

- Worship invokes His presence. "God inhabits the praises of His people."
- and many more ...

We've even had people saved, and had miracles happen during our worship times without even giving any invitation for them! When people worship, stuff happens!

Expressions of Worship

Below is a inconclusive list of different expressions of worship. It's important to note that any, or even all, these expressions may be displayed by someone, but if the heart doesn't engage, true worship never happened.

Worship is a "heart thing!"
- Singing
- Declaring
- Verbalized praise
- Praising in tongues
- Reading the Word aloud
- Shouting
- Whispering
- Standing
- Bowing down
- Kneeling
- Laying prostrate
- Outstretched hands
- Uplifted hands
- Clapping hands
- Dancing
- Swaying
- Weeping
- Laughing
- Stillness
- Quietness/Loudness

While many of these expressions may be way off the map for you today, it's highly possible they won't be as you evolve into your role as a true worshiper! "But God demonstrates His own love toward us, in that Jesus died for us when we were still sinners" (Romans 5:8). Seeing how the Father has so extravagantly demonstrated His love for us, doesn't it make perfect sense that we would find extravagant ways to express our gratefulness to Him? How do you express your love to Him?

Leaders

It's extremely rare for any congregation to exceed the leaders' commitment to worship. In that sense, the pastor is the worship leader. He may be like me and not be able to sing a lick, play an instrument, or ever be on a worship team. His commitment to worship is extremely important in the overall scheme of worship in the church. During one of our worship services, the Lord spoke to me, "Andy, the most noble and honorable thing you can do is to bring a family of true worshipers to Me!" As leaders, it's our responsibility to cultivate the environment necessary for our people to be able to engage in a deep worship experience with the Father.

True Worshipers

True worshipers are those who are developing a deeper love for the Father. They have a passion to love Him and a determination to show that love by giving Him the praise He deserves. True worshipers hearts are overflowing with their devotion to God. True worshipers understand they have unrestricted access to God, and they're learning to make the best of it! They have made the ultimate sacrifice: Rom 12:1-3 - "I beseech you therefore, brethren, by the mercies of God, that you present your bodies a living sacrifice, holy, acceptable to God, which is your reasonable service. And do not be conformed to this world, but be transformed by the renewing of your mind, that you may prove what is that good and acceptable and perfect will of God." True worshipers don't just worship on Sunday. Their very lives, and all they do, are an expression of worship to the Father!

"Unrestricted Access"

You see the passes at most every public event, especially the big ones; "All Access." The placard, usually worn around a person's neck is an indicator for every official on the grounds of the event that anyone wearing this placard can go anywhere they want to go, and at any time. Those "All Access" passes also

> carry the often unsaid understanding that the wearers are obviously of some importance. You know, like a real VIP!
>
> The person wearing that "All Access" pass must've evidently been given a level of trust not offered to everyone. With that particular pass comes some extra responsibility, too, I'd say. Take a rock concert, for example. Let's say Bob Seger (one of my faves, especially since I can't go see Tom Petty anymore) is performing at Red Rocks in Colorado. Now, that'd be a great combo; great entertainment at a great venue. If you have one of those "All Access" passes, you might get to be up close and personal with Bob Seger himself. I'll bet you could even get your picture taken with him and the band if you were really lucky. But, without that "All Access" pass, it ain't gonna happen! But, most of us are resigned to just go to the concert and enjoy the entertainment from a distance. Nothing wrong with that, whatsoever. But, it's just not the same as having the VIP treatment.
>
> The One Who created the Universe has given you an "All Access" pass to be in His presence anytime it strikes your fancy. There's never a bouncer at the door, no one checking ID's, nobody deciding if you have the correct credentials. No one is there to turn you away because you don't have the right clearance; nobody to stamp your hand in case you go out and want to come back in. You don't even have to show your "All Access" pass! They "all" know who you are! Nope, nothing, whatsoever, to keep you from engaging in conversation, face to face worship, fellowship, and communion with God, Himself! Think about that for a minute!
>
> It's true! You've been given (because we couldn't earn it!) unrestricted access to God! That's a BIG DEAL!
>
> Question is, what are you gonna do about it?"
>
> *This and more thoughts from Andy can be found at his blog: "The Way I See It" - www.andyrtaylor.com.*

Conclusion

One thing I've learned through the years is that the enemy hates worship. It reminds him of what he gave up. Oh, he doesn't mind a song service, one that's not done from the heart. When it comes to true worship, he'll do anything he can to disrupt and ultimately destroy it, if he's able to. We've had so many challenges and roadblocks, but we have remained focused on what the Father has told us. We're committed to true worship. I said years ago, "If I have to lead worship with a cookie sheet and a wooden spoon, we were still going to do it." So far, gratefully, it hasn't come to that! Let's make a commitment to true worship so we can remove it from *The Best Kept Secrets In The Kingdom*.

PLAN OF ACTION:

- Draw nearer to the Father
- Spend some time just resting in His presence
- Learn to express your love to Him
- Worship publicly (in church) and privately
- Take the awesome opportunity to become a true worshiper
- Find and listen to some of the well-known worship leaders
- Tell the Lord, "I love You!" often!

LEADERS:

- Deepen in your devotion to the Father
- You are the worship leader!
- Communicate the vision for worship to your worship people
- Set the bar up high for worship
- Teach/nurture your people to be true worshipers
- Contend for the presence of God in your gatherings
- Allow the Lord to take you/your people into deeper levels of worship

PRAY:

"Father, I desire to worship You in ways that bring honor to You. Help me to be a true worshiper."

RESOURCES:

- *Extravagant Worship* by Darlene Zschech
- *How To Worship a King* by Zach Neese
- *To Know You More* by Andy Park
- *The Hallelujah Factor* by Jack R. Taylor

What Is the Lord Saying?

"Man shall not live by bread alone but by every word that proceeds out of the mouth of God" (Luke 4:4).
—Jesus

Seems like a simple enough question, but in my experience, it's clearly to be included in *The Best Kept Secrets In The Kingdom*. Even a novice in understanding church customs and practices knows the most important thing for any leader is to get a read on what the Lord is saying. Working with some of those churches and leaders, I've found it to be a pretty rare occurrence.

I became friends with a pastor in another state some years back. Seminary trained, he had been quite successful, at least in terms of the phenomenal growth of his church. He had taken the church, which at the time had a couple of hundred people, and under his leadership had grown to over 1700 in just ten years. Impressive by anyone's standards. He was one of the best I've seen at studying, researching, organizing and even delivering a well-crafted sermon. He accompanied me on a ministry trip to one of the churches connected with us. It was a good time to swap ministry stories and get to know one another. This friend had a lot of Bible knowledge and took great pride in his preaching ability but in our conversation confessed that he had heard plenty of pastors talk about the things they'd heard from the Lord. In his honesty he admitted that he didn't think he'd ever heard anything from the Lord, himself. I was shocked. I'm sure the look on my face gave away the thoughts that were running through my mind. He went on to say he didn't know how to start to do that and asked if I could help him in the process. I agreed to do so, but it's proof that one can go a long way preaching, and even leading, without actually hearing what the Lord is saying. In my mind, it's a serious infraction and an obvious departure from Kingdom values.

Another pastor from a small town brought a couple of his leaders to spend a few days with us to talk about their church, what the circumstances and challenges were and where they might need help. Early on in our conversation, I asked the pastor what he felt like the Lord has said to him about the church. He proceeded to tell me the things they were doing in terms of training, evangelism and outreach. I asked him again, "What has the Lord said?" Again, he went on to say how they were addressing certain facets of the church. I asked again with more emphasis, "What has the Lord said?" He started again telling me about one thing then another. This time I cut him off, which is way off the map of how I operate on a normal basis. On top of that I was quite louder and much more animated than usual. I did sense the leadership of the Holy Spirit and felt this particular situation warranted my response. I grabbed him by the shoulders, looked square into his eyes and said, "I'm not asking you what you're doing! I'm asking what you've heard from the Lord?" For a second or two it was pretty uncomfortable for the few of us in the room. I said, "We want to help you as much as we can, but your church isn't going to be successful because we're great at giving the right counsel and instruction. Your church is going to be successful, only, if you're determined and desperate to hear the Lord!" They got the point. Now, they lead a thriving church in what I'd call a tough region. They're making great inroads into the community, not because we gave good advice, although I think we did. They're being effective because they've put the priority on hearing the voice of the Lord concerning the specifics of their church. Very recently, I had a phone conversation with this pastor, and in it, he told of ministering to someone, and he asked them, "What's the Lord saying to you?" Mission accomplished!

These are just two stories of many others that reveal what I would call a serious issue in the church today. You can bet if hearing the Lord isn't a high priority for a leader, it's certainly not going to be very important to their people. It might well be the main reason that the church in America in some places is floundering, ineffective, and without clear direction. Being the only non-denominational church in our town, we have undergone a great deal of scrutiny and criticism in teaching people the importance and simplicity of hearing the Lord.

Some of the younger men in our church became disenchanted with me a few years back. These were guys I loved very much, had invested in, and saw as "sons" in the Lord. Their problem came about as they would come to me with a dilemma going on in their life. Their expectation was for me to analyze their situation and tell them exactly what they should do. To their dismay, I didn't do that. What I did do was ask them the question, "What's the Lord telling you?" They confessed later their disappointment in me for not giving them a solution. I think they might even admit they were furious with me, at least momentarily. At the time, they felt I was neglecting my duties as a pastor or father in the Lord and just passing the buck. But they made a revolutionary discovery. They found out that the

Lord was as eager to talk to them about their problems as they were eager for a solution! They will tell you today that it's one of the most valuable things I've done for them. I routinely hear them now asking someone else who has brought their problems to them, "What's the Lord telling you?"

When the opportunity presented itself to buy the property where the church is now located, I walked on the property, asking the Lord what we should do. In that still, small voice I felt the Lord posed a question to me, "Does it take more faith to buy it or not to buy it?" Well, that was an easy answer. The problem was we had virtually no money. To complicate the decision another party wanted to buy the property and they were financially healthy enough to do it. They did say if they bought the property we could use the building we were having services in. The next thing the Lord said was, "Do you want other people making your faith decisions for you?" Again, the answer seemed very clear. We decided to buy. I went to the bank and told our banker we wanted to buy the property. I asked for a month to cast the vision to our people. In August of 1997 we had a Sunday we were going to give toward the purchase of the property. At the time, the demographics of our church were pretty much middle to lower-income people. On that Sunday we had $30,000 cash come in and another $45,000 committed over the next year. In two short years we had totally paid off the property! I still say if you went back and looked at the means of our people and their ability to give that it wouldn't make sense. It was totally a supernatural thing that happened. That's what happens when a priority is put on hearing the Lord.

It's a fact that the Father wants to talk to His kids. Jesus even said, "My sheep know Me, and they hear My voice." While it's a serious issue, I often jokingly tell people that if they're not hearing the Lord, chances are the problem's not on His end. If you think about it from a practical standpoint, it just makes sense that every father wants to communicate with his kids. God, the Father, is a much better parent than we are, so we know He loves to talk to us.

It seems the problem arises for some when they hear another person say something they've heard from the Lord. They automatically think we're talking about hearing Him in an audible voice. While I know plenty of people who believe they've heard the audible voice of God, and I do believe them, He has never spoken to me in that way. I'm sure open to it, but so far it hasn't happened. God is not limited in the ways He can speak to us. I have also found that He speaks to each of us in unique ways. For instance, you might be one who has lots of dreams. Or maybe He uses numbers and imagery in how He speaks to you. You are uniquely made and special to the Father, so you can expect Him to speak to you in ways that are very personal to you.

There are many ways God speaks. For starters, it's vital to understand that God speaks through the Written Word. When I hear someone complain they're not hearing anything from the Lord, I always ask, "Are you getting in the Word?" More often than not, the answer is "No." In fact, I do believe that there are times the Lord will be silent on all the other ways He might speak just so we'll return to the Book! I think that's extremely important. He loves to speak to our hearts through what is "written!" I've written a book called Reading Your Bible For All Its Worth. People have found it to be very helpful in simplifying, understanding, and enjoying their Bible. But the sad truth is many believers today don't put the priority on digging in the Word to find their own answers. Those who put out the effort find quickly that the Holy Spirit is there to help and He (the Spirit) is quick to touch our hearts and "highlight," or illuminate those issues He wants to bring alive to us. The written Word is also our standard of Truth. It's there to help us understand some of the other ways in which He speaks. God never contradicts Himself. So, no matter how He chooses to speak to you in ways other than the Bible, if what you think you've heard is inconsistent with what's written, it cannot be God.

Below are some of the other ways the Father speaks to His children:
- Audibly
- Dreams
- Visions
- Words of Knowledge
- Words of Wisdom
- Prophecy
- Through our circumstances
- Through other people
- Nature
- Numbers
- Signs and wonders
- and my very favorite: The "still small voice"

This is not an exhaustive list by any means, but you get the point.

If we're going to make hearing God a priority, we may have to deal with some of our preconceived ideas and faulty thought patterns. For instance, if you've been in a church environment that says God doesn't speak anymore, and you've bought into that, you probably won't hear Him either. It's actually a self-fulfilling prophecy. Those who declare God doesn't speak anymore hear absolutely nothing from Him! Others may have the opinion that God only speaks to the elite, or those who are super spiritual. Again, not the case at all but those schools of thought are out there. It seems clear that we should boil it down to the simplest element: God is a Father, and fathers want to communicate with their children! Don't over-complicate it! Keep it simple.

Amos prophesied generations ago about an impending famine. "Behold, the days are coming," says the Lord, "That I will send a famine on the land, Not famine of bread, Nor a thirst for water, But of hearing the words of the Lord." I'm not at all suggesting that we are living in the age he referred to, but there is, even today, a famine of hearing the words of the Lord. I would go further to say it's not a God induced famine but a famine caused by the failure on the part of leaders not putting the priority where it should be. In the final analysis I would encourage you to make hearing the Lord a priority. As a son or daughter you're on a need-to-know basis with the Father. So, use your faith. You'll miss Him and what He's saying to you, much less than you think you will.

I've learned by following the Father that He always knows the right thing to say, and always at just the right time. That being said, I love to tell people that they're on a need-to-know basis with the Lord. Everything you need to know, in perfect timing, is there for you at all times. If you think about it, that gives us an unbelievable advantage in everything we do.

Let's agree together that hearing the Lord is something we all need to do, and maybe we can move it off the list of *The Best Kept Secrets In The Kingdom*.

PLAN OF ACTION:

- Make it a priority to hear the Lord
- Adjust your prayer time to include some "listening"
- Become acquainted with the voice of the Lord as He has unique ways of speaking to each of us
- Write down the things you believe you've heard from the Lord
- Pray and declare those things

LEADERS:

- If you're going to lead, you MUST put a priority on hearing the Lord
- If it's not a priority to you, it won't be a priority for your people
- People have a desire to follow those who are saying what God's saying
- Help simplify hearing the Lord for your people
- Instructing on hearing the Lord should be one of the first things we teach a new convert. *It will set the tone for the rest of their lives!

PRAY:

"Father, give me a hunger to hear Your voice."

Ministry to The Poor

"Blessed is he who considers the poor; The Lord will deliver him in time of trouble. The Lord will preserve him and keep him alive, And he will be blessed on the earth" (Ps. 41:1-2).
—David

Interestingly enough, you won't find any Biblical reference for government agencies taking care of the poor. You will find plenty of evidence for the church to do so. You'll find many verses in the Bible, similar to the one above. It's obvious that ministry to the poor is a very important part of the overall picture of ministry altogether. Have you noticed that Jesus always kept company with the poor. It's clear He enjoyed His time with them much more than he did with the over-religious, self-righteous doctrinal police, the Pharisees. There was something about Jesus that made them feel significant. Around Jesus, they felt like they could "make it!" He didn't just accept them. He loved them and valued them. The atmosphere around Jesus was 100% charged with agape, and they were drawn into it. If we can capture this in the church today, the results will be staggering, to say the least.

When we started in Sayre, the first thing I heard from the Lord was, "Andy, I want you to start praying that I would bring you the people nobody else wants." It's a sad state of affairs, but in reality, there are a lot of people out there that the church doesn't really want. Why would the church not want them? Well, for starters, they're not givers; they have baggage; they require a lot of time and effort; many are "problem people" that are often extremely hard to deal with, etc. The list could go on and on. Even with all that considered it should still be a priority of the church in any generation. We did start praying as the Lord directed and have been faithfully doing so for over 30 years. God has taken the "people nobody wanted" and changed them into people that everybody wants! That's what happens when you make ministry to the poor a priority!

I started to school in a little small town in Western Oklahoma in 1959 just a few days before turning six years old. It was about a ten mile ride on the school bus picking up all the country kids. On the bus that first day was a little girl about my age who got on the bus. Her little dress was dirty. Her hands and feet had dirt stains on them and her little shoes were all but worn out. I remember coming home from school that day and cried as I told my Mom about the little girl. It turned out that the family lived in a house not far from us with a dirt floor, no running water and no indoor bathroom facilities. I was broken-hearted for that little girl and for her family. It has now been roughly 60 years from that day and I've never gotten over it. Even as I write today the tears come easy. I don't say that to commend myself; far from it. I say it because, looking back, it revealed a place in my heart that the Father created to have empathy for the less fortunate. It's how the Lord made me. It took me many years before I realized that. I have always been very protective of those in my circle who were poor and neglected. Kids can be very cruel. One of the things that hurt me the deepest is when kids were getting picked on who didn't have a dad living in the home. It got me in trouble with the bigger kids more times than I can remember as I tried to "take up" for the victim. Looking back, I guess the thought of them having no defender was more than I could take. Because of that I found myself in the company of the down-and-outers most of my life. To be honest many of that crowd down through the years have become some of my closest friends. I believe we all have God-given traits that are like Jesus. Even though I didn't understand it until later in life, I think my heart for the poor is a gift—a very valuable gift—and one that I treasure deeply these days. There is, however, a downside for those with a heart for the poor. People like me are an easy target for those with an "entitlement" attitude who are bent on working and beating the system. I'll be the first to admit my ability to discern those with legitimate needs from the "users" in the world is weak, to state it mildly.

It was a natural thing when we started in Sayre to have an active ministry to the poor. Because we started with a little group of about six to eight people, the resources were very limited. It never failed; whatever the need was, we always had enough to help. We became *known as a church that would help anyone. We had some of the other churches in our town and even a few from surrounding towns refer those needing help to us. I can't help but believe they saw them as a liability while we always saw them as an asset. Over the years, the Lord has seen to it that we've always had enough resources to help. I don't know of anyone else doing it but we even paid a part-time salary to one of our men. His only job description: Go out and find people who need help! While we now have a full time paid staff member whose chief job is to deal with all types of benevolence issues it doesn't absolve each individual's responsibility to meet some of those needs as they arise. "It's more blessed to give than to receive." It's only when we put that to the test by actually giving that we experience the truth of it!

I've said for years, "The poor in America need the church but not nearly as much as the church needs the poor." That statement draws plenty of curiosity from those hearing it. Let me explain. Anytime you are confronted with someone in need and you have resources it's an indicator of the condition of your heart. In fact, I believe it's one of the clearest indicators. It's like one of those "Your Are Here" signs in the mall. It's a very good thing to have the condition, and attitude of our heart revealed to us, both individually and corporately. When we find that our willingness to help those in need is lacking or absent altogether, it's a great time to make that important heart adjustment. I sincerely believe it's one of those things that most needs to be fixed in the American church. Almost everyone agrees that ministry to the poor is important. Experience has taught me that most people would rather give to someone doing it, than to actually do it themselves. It's easy to understand why. From a church leader's standpoint, ministry to the poor isn't easy. It takes someone heading up the ministry with the right heart but who is also street smart, and that can discern the needs that are legitimate.

A family moved here from a couple of hours away in Texas. After being here for a few years and "catching" the DNA of our house, they planned to move back to their town of about 30,000 and launch into ministry. The husband asked me what I thought he should do in terms of ministry when he settled back there. I answered, "First, I would find out who the poor are in your community and how you might be able to serve them to meet their needs." He asked, "Why would you do that?" My answer, "Because if you'll figure out how to minister to the poor, God will bless every other thing you do." Who are the poor? It makes sense to determine who the poor are in your community. It would obviously include those with limited resources as well as those society has shunned. It might just be the rich man who has money and possessions but is in a lost and depressed state. At any rate, it is wise to do a little legwork to find out "who" they are, where they congregate and what their needs are.

Stopped dead in my tracks!

I had jokingly made the statement a hundred times throughout the years, "If I were in Cowboy Stadium, 90,000 people, and there was one 'nut case' there, he'll find me!" It has actually been the case my whole life. A few years ago I made that statement and the Lord stopped me dead in my tracks! He said, "I know, Andy. That's a gift I've given you. I don't trust those people with just anybody!" It was a revelation that cut me to the heart. I did an immediate "about-face!" It changed me forever! So, if you're one of those who has experienced a similar phenomenon, congratulations! As uncomfortable as it might be at the start the Lord wants to use you to love that segment of society. I would almost go so far to say that if your heart is correct, you won't have to look for them. They'll find you!

The poor hold a special place in the heart of Jesus. John the Baptist, in prison and soon to be put to death, sent two of his followers to check Jesus out, "Are you the One, or should we look for another?" Jesus, who never took the bait to try and prove Himself, answered, "Go tell John the things which you hear and see: The blind see and the lame walk; the lepers are cleansed, and the deaf hear; the dead are raised up, and the poor have the gospel preached to them." Included in the list of supernatural works, Jesus didn't neglect to mention the poor!

Unless we're doing something to help the poor, we're neglecting one of the most important ingredients of the New Testament church. In James' short letter he writes, "Don't you know that God has chosen the poor in this world to be rich in faith?" From this verse we could easily conclude that there is powerful spiritual potential residing in the poor in our communities and virtually no one is contending for them! There are great blessings awaiting those who do! Obviously, it's another of *The Best Kept Secrets In The Kingdom*.

"Known"

One of the things that frequently come my way as a pastor is the performing of funerals. It's amazing what the Lord has done; when I was a young man, I'd avoid going to them at all because of the feeling that it left me with. But soon after I was in the ministry, I got my first request to do one. I immediately thought, "There's no way!" Even though I said yes, I wasn't sure I could do it. But I found that the Lord had given me the grace to do it, and I made it through the first one. Since that time, I've done over 400 more funerals. It's always an honor to be asked to do a service, but it carries with it a good size load of stress. I figure, compared to the grieving family, I've got the easy part.

I recently got a call from the funeral home to do a service. I didn't recognize the name of the woman, but I said yes, anyway. I was sure that I'd know someone in the family, but after reading the obituary, I, again, didn't recognize anyone. I met with the family the next day to plan the service, and I was sure I'd know at least one of them. Nope, didn't know any of them, either. It was apparent that the family didn't have many resources; the cardboard casket was just more evidence of that. On the day of the funeral, I asked the funeral director if he knew this family, to which he said, "No." I told him that I didn't know them either, to which he replied, "Well, they know you!" and "They specifically asked for you!"

I can't explain in words how that made me feel. It's one thing to be 'known' in the company of the "elite," and I guess I have a few acquaintances in that small crowd. It's a totally different thing to be 'known' in the community of the downtrodden! I can't remember when anything left me feeling more honored than that!

This and more thoughts from Andy can be found at his blog: "The Way I See It" - www.andyrtaylor.com.

PLAN OF ACTION:

- Do a personal heart check and make any needed adjustments
- Ask the Lord to "up" your awareness of those around you who need help
- Look for and do the right thing when the opportunity arises

LEADERS:

- Develop a plan to help the poor in your community
- Begin to be an "advocate" for the poor and impart it to your people
- Encourage the whole church to monitor their own heart
- Seek out those who have a heart for ministry to the poor
- Empower them to develop their ministry
- Set aside funds exclusively to help the poor

PRAY:

*"Father, enlarge my heart for the poor.
Thank You for opportunities to help those less fortunate."*

Understanding Grace

"If you want to make people mad preach the Law;
if you want to make them furious, preach grace!"
—Unknown

It's crazy but true! It has never been more true than in recent religious history, unless, of course, you had been around during the first century. Because of its profound importance, and in light of the many misunderstandings compounded by those who inaccurately teach grace, it's vital to be put on the list of *The Best Kept Secrets In The Kingdom*.

A luncheon was held more than a half-century ago in England. The general topic was comparative religions, which sparked a debate on the question of Christianity's most valuable distinction. What separated Christianity from every other religion in the world? C.S. Lewis, who joined to debate, uttered the answer as soon as he heard the topic, "'Oh, that's easy,' said perhaps the greatest apologist of the twentieth century. 'It's grace.'"

I've been a grace man since November 17, 1984. That's the night I sat on the edge of my bed weeping, with everything wrong in my life that could be wrong, and said to the Lord, "God, if you're out there, You gotta help me." He had absolutely no good reason to answer that desperate plea for me, but He did it anyway! That, my friend, is grace in a nutshell: God's unmerited, unearned favor expressed through His unconditional, immeasurable and limitless love. The next days, weeks, months, and now years since then, the Father has done nothing but to strengthen and fortify His goodness, and His grace toward me.

The Grace Controversy

Grace has become one of the most controversial topics facing believers in our generation. I've noticed that anything that draws such attention usually has some very important ramifications for all of us. If we're willing to chill out, not get involved in the fray, search the Scriptures, allow them to change our mind (if needed), and ask the Lord for clarification, it all becomes crystal clear. So far, that hasn't happened on the larger scale. As a result, much of the Body of Christ has been divided, fragmented and polarized with neither side giving up much ground. Both sides of the argument present valid points, and the truth is somewhere in the middle. In an attempt to diffuse the controversy, even if it's on a small scale, I'll share:

1. Why is grace so controversial?
2. Solutions to the controversy
3. Living with one another in the meantime.

Why the controversy?

For starters, it may be new to you, but this controversy over grace is not a new thing. It has been going on since Jesus came to earth. If you want to lay the blame on someone, start there. He initiated the New Covenant, a covenant of grace. That started the firestorm of controversy with the Jews because it was an affront to their Law. Now, you have to give them some grace here. (pun intended!) Since the Law had been their guide for many generations and they'd heard absolutely nothing about grace, it would be normal for them to dig their heels in upon hearing the words of Jesus, especially since it was so diametrically opposed to their mindset at the time. They not only dug their heels in; they wanted to kill anyone talking about grace starting with Jesus. Jesus says clearly, "I didn't come to destroy the Law but to fulfill it" (Matt. 5:17). That's one of the main points of argument, among several others, with those fighting against the grace message today. Jesus DID come to fulfill the Law. He did that because we couldn't do it. No man could keep the Law. Even for one trying to keep the Law, if he fails in even one little facet of it, he's guilty of violating all of it! No man was ever made righteous by the Law. It couldn't happen. So, because of that, Jesus did keep the Law, and in keeping it, He fulfilled it! The Bible is crystal clear; we're no longer under the Law but under grace.

The controversy is also fueled by those who preach grace without actually walking in grace, themselves. When I hear a "grace preacher" condemning, criticizing, and belittling anyone who's not in total agreement with them and their theories, I immediately think, "You're talking grace, but you're not giving grace!" That just feels bad! It shouldn't be happening! When the grace message is not accompanied with an attitude of grace toward others, the message is severely contaminated. It's no wonder the detractors of grace pitch a fit. Who could blame them? When grace is adequately and clearly communicated, very few people reject it! The argument over grace these days really comes down to the one side saying God's not as good as the other side says He is. So, for those preaching grace, make sure you're walking in it or stop talking about it. You're adding to the problem!

Solutions to the Controversy

For starters, let's just give one another some space. Without going into full "war" mode with those we disagree with let's listen to the other side. Maybe they'll even listen to you as well. Healthy dialogue is helpful for everyone willing to engage in the process. Understanding the difference between the Old and New Covenants is a must in coming to sensible conclusions about grace. Of course, there's no substitute for careful and systematic study of the Scriptures to gain a deeper, clearer perspective. Those things, coupled with a heart that is willing to change and adapt, guarantee we will continue to grow and evolve in our understanding of grace and into the image of Jesus.

Living With One Another in the Meantime

I was having a phone conversation with a great friend. We both agreed we weren't in exactly the same place on the subject of grace. We didn't argue the point. Instead, we honored one another's different views on the subject. It was healthy. In the end I summed it up this way; "Here's what I know." "You're after God, and so am I." "If we keep doing that, this time next year I won't be here, and you won't be there." "We'll both be in a different place where grace is concerned." If we can learn to live with one another while the Holy Spirit guides us into all truth we'll all be better off for it. It's just how it should work in the Kingdom.

Hyper-Grace?

It's a phrase that has arisen out of the whole grace controversy. The label doesn't do much to dispel the argument. In fact, it actually helps to incite it to a fever pitch. The paragraph below is taken from a Christian website and is typical of the accusations leveled at anyone teaching and preaching grace. While some of the points are valid, most are what I'd term as falling far on the side of "radical" teachings on grace. Radical, extreme teachings are found just about everywhere and in just about every form of religion. There are those radical teachers of grace out there, but there are also very many more who are sound and correct in their teaching on it. As a grace person myself, I don't hold to the final conclusions as communicated below. Based on this paragraph, I'm not a hyper-grace teacher at all. But I am, unequivocally, a grace teacher! At any rate, it's up to each of us to apply ourselves to understand grace and its full ramifications as we look at "the whole counsel of God," and we strive to divide the word of truth rightly.

Our lives are to be lived in a delicate balance (only brought about by the Holy Spirit!) between liberty and responsibility.

> "The term hyper-grace has been used to describe a new wave of teaching that emphasizes the grace of God to the exclusion of other vital teachings such as repentance and confession of sin. Hyper-grace teachers maintain that all sin, past, present, and future, has already been forgiven, so there is no need for a believer ever to confess it. Hyper-grace teaching says that, when God looks at us, He sees only a holy and righteous people. The conclusion of hyper-grace teaching is that we are not bound by Jesus' teaching, even as we are not under the Law; that believers are not responsible for their sin; and that anyone who disagrees is a pharisaical legalist."

Statements and conclusions like this one have caused many to shy away from any teachings on grace, whatsoever. It's a tragic phenomenon, as I see it. As a result, most are satisfied to remain in limbo and have resolved to be okay with hearing a mixture of law and grace. As the old saying goes, "Don't throw the baby out with the bathwater." Detractors of the grace message erroneously conclude that when we say we're not under the Law we are saying it's okay to be careless when it comes to sin. I've not heard anyone say that, and I honestly don't know anyone who even thinks like that. It's ludicrous to assume that of those who are beginning to understand grace. It is an unfair assumption, to say the very least. Those ascribing to a deeper level of grace understand that living under grace does not free one from moral obligation. Give grace another look and seek to find your own balance in it. Heads up! You're likely to be labeled a heretic when you do. You're in good company, though. They did the same with Jesus.

Mixture—A Deadly Potion

Paul's letter to the Galatians gives a perfect example of mixture. The Judaizers (born again Jews who still erroneously believed one should keep the Law) were pressuring the new Gentile believers saying they must be circumcised and keep the Jewish Law. Paul, in his desire to be correct made a trip to Jerusalem to meet with the apostles and elders there to decide this extremely important issue. It was decided there that the Gentiles were NOT required to keep the Law. The "centerpiece" verse of his letter to the Galatians states: "Stand fast, therefore, in the liberty wherewith Christ has made you free, and don't be entangled again in a yoke of bondage" (Galatians

5:1). Most people think Paul was referring to sin when he talks about a "yoke of bondage." But He's not talking about sin as we would normally describe it. He's passionately telling the Galatians not get entangled in the same form of dead religion he had been tangled up in earlier, himself!

Most of what the church population hears these days, especially in the Bible Belt, is a mixture of law and grace. Mixing law with grace dilutes the message of grace and renders it ineffective in its ability to produce the dramatic results in a believer's life the Father has intended. Those who practice this type of ministry somehow believe adding law to grace causes the message to have "teeth" in it as to scare people into thinking they're never really "all right" with God. Evidently they think this is a good way to produce righteous behavior. It's not! It has at its very root, condemnation, "the act of making someone feel bad, so they'll do something good" (my own definition). You won't find Jesus doing it this way. Why should we think it would be a viable method today?!

Most people think that personal holiness is brought about by an awareness of sin in their life. That couldn't be further from the truth. True holiness is brought about by an awareness of the goodness of God, as only understood by experiencing it firsthand. When we see, or better yet experience, the goodness of God on a personal basis, it causes us to "want to" change for the better. In that way, we're not changing because someone is telling us how bad we are and of all the things we need to change to get God to like us more. As we "taste and see" the goodness of God and understand that He already loves us with a perfect, flawless, and unconditional love, we want to start to bring our life into line with Him. An accurate understanding of grace always leads to less sin in a person's life, never more! Romans 2:4 "It is the goodness of God that leads us to repentance." Anyone teaching a mixture of law and grace isn't teaching grace at all!

Charles Spurgeon, one of the great spiritual minds of long ago addressed mixture in no uncertain terms.

> "We sing, and rightly too—"My soul, no more attempt to draw Thy life and comfort from the law ... for from the law death comes and not life, misery, and not comfort. To convince and to condemn is all the law can do. When will all professors, and especially all professed ministers of Christ, learn the difference between the law and the gospel? Most of them make a mingle-mangle and serve out deadly potions to the people, often containing but

one ounce of gospel to a pound of law, whereas, but even a grain of law is enough to spoil the whole thing."

There wasn't a more staunch proponent of the Law in the first century than Paul. He was a Jew's Jew by anyone's standards. His mission in life was to see these Jesus people dragged in before the courts, judged to be guilty and stoned to death as their punishment. He had a zeal for the Lord, but not according to knowledge. Everything changed for him when he had an encounter with Jesus. His conversion was as dramatic as any you'll find in the Bible. One day he was all about killing the grace people and, literally the next day, he was one of them! From that day forward, until his death, he was the greatest communicator on the planet for the cause of grace. His message caused him to be ostracized by his countrymen, maybe even some of his own family members. He was beaten a few times, once so bad he was even left for dead. Every letter he penned started and ended with grace. No one was more qualified than Paul to talk about grace. He had experienced both the Law and now grace. As much as he loved the Jewish Law, he gave it all up and counted it as rubbish as compared to the grace and love he found in Jesus. Once he experienced his own relationship with Jesus and the grace He offered, Paul was never the same. While the details, times, and conditions were different, it was the same for me, and it can be the same for you. Grace, when understood, will totally transform your life from the "inside out!"

Living in the "Finished Work of Jesus"

As Jesus drew His last breaths on the cross, He uttered, "It is finished." Every single thing He came to the earth to do had been completed. The Law had been fulfilled. He laid down His life. His blood was shed. He arose from the grave. The New Covenant had been ratified and was now in full effect.

The Bible Belt: "The Land of Never Enough"

After many years in the ministry, there are things you start to notice, things that stand out. There are patterns of thought and behavior that seem to be deeply woven into the fabric of Bible Belt mentality. One such pattern that runs very deep among born again believers is that one can never do enough to get, or stay, in good standing with God. If you wonder why I say that, here's why. I hear it all the time:

"I don't go to church enough,"
"I don't pray enough,"
"I don't read the Bible enough,"
"I don't have enough faith," "I'm not a very good Christian,"
"I hope I'm going to heaven."

I just heard this from a man yesterday, "I think God has given up on me." I refuted that lie as quick as I could!

It's a prevalent attitude with many people always thinking they can never do enough or be good enough to satisfy the Lord. It gives the feeling they're trying to serve a God that's unreasonably demanding and impossible to please. It's like being on a treadmill of performance in an effort to earn their own righteousness; A state, in fact, many never seem to arrive at. This is a problem of the highest order, in my opinion, because it gives an incorrect image of "Who" God actually is. It's one of the greatest misrepresentations the world has ever seen. There are many out there who'll live their entire lives believing they were never quite acceptable or good enough to please God. What's worse, it leads one to believe the Father's love is based entirely on our behavior.

Sad, Sad, Sad!

What's on your list of things to do that make you righteous? While you're at it, explain to me where the line is of, enough, or not enough. Truth is, if you never read your Bible, if you never went to church your righteousness isn't diminished one bit. I'm not advocating that, just pointing it out! You're not righteous because of the things you do; you're righteous because of what He did! The Father doesn't love you because you're good; He loves you because He's good!

THAT, in itself, makes me want to do good!

Good fathers would never keep their children in limbo over such important things! So, pack your bags, shred your list, enjoy your relationship with the Father, and get out of the land of never enough!

I often hear people confessing, "I'm just an old sinner saved by grace". I have serious issues with that line of thinking! We were sinners, but not anymore since we've been born again. Born again of incorruptible seed, the Book says! Noted Bible teacher Bob Mumford says it this way:

"All the DNA of the oak tree is in a single little acorn."

If you're born again the "seed" of righteousness has been germinated in you. Through our relationship, fellowship and, ultimately, our union with the Father that little seed will grow to full stature as we're being conformed into the image of Jesus. So, no! You're not a sinner anymore! Stop confessing it! When you begin to understand grace, your attitude, conduct, and behavior will come into line with your true identity.

Grace is an extremely important subject because how you perceive grace will largely dictate how you see God. It will heavily influence how you see others and how you relate to them in the course of your life. Grace understood, reveals the incredible, magnificent goodness of God. They don't call it the "good news" for nothing!

God is good! The more you understand His grace, the more you'll realize just how good He is!

There's Grace For That!

I catch myself saying that quite a bit these days. I say it because it's true. And it doesn't matter what the situation or circumstances are—it's always true—without fail. We had one of our young couples recently who miscarried. It's a devastating event. She was a little life so looked forward to, anticipated and planned for. Little brothers and sisters were excited about their new sibling. Grandparents, aunts, and uncles had already been shopping for the new little one. Then, all of a sudden, the stunning, paralyzing news came. I hurt deeply for the young couple because I know all too well the pain and heartbreak that naturally ensues. That grief that comes is not proof that something's wrong with us. No! Much to the contrary, it's proof that something's 'right' with us! We've been there, done that, and somehow lived through it. The reason we lived is because there's grace for that!

I just talked to a couple of brothers last night who had just, unexpectedly, lost their dad. He was in the hospital, serious but improving, then all of a sudden he's gone. I don't have anything to compare to it. I know that it's one of those things that has the potential to hit the heart in the deepest place. I can't help but be broken for my friends, but they'll be OK. They'll be OK 'cause there's grace for that too!

A young guy was in my office today. His wife had just informed him that she doesn't love him anymore. He's devastated; he has no answers, and his heart is broken in two. What's going to happen with the kids? How can he explain this nightmare to them? There's grace for that too! Somehow the Father and the grace that He freely gives will see them all through!

> It doesn't have to be a tragedy for grace to appear; whenever, however, and for whatever grace is needed, it's always there. There's always enough of it. The Father knows what you need, and He won't keep you waiting!
>
> Whatever you're going through right now and whatever you need right now. There's Grace For That!
>
> *This and more thoughts from Andy can be found at his blog: "The Way I See It" - www.andyrtaylor.com.*

PLAN OF ACTION:

- Do your own due diligence on the subject of grace
- Allow the Holy Spirit to shape your understanding
- Be willing to change your mind as the Spirit matures you
- Look at Jesus—He's the perfect picture of grace
- Most important: Interact with the Father so you will have firsthand knowledge of grace! Taste and see that the Lord, He is good!
- Open your heart to the possibility that Jesus has already done it "all" for you
- Avoid arguing over grace

LEADERS:

- Engage in an exhaustive study on grace
- Be cautious not to teach a mixture of law and grace
- Walk-in grace toward others
- Be methodical, thorough and deliberate in teaching grace to your people
- Be ready to address the controversy in an edifying, life-giving way
- Step in and mediate arguments over grace to bring edification

PRAY:

"Father, open the eyes of my understanding where grace is concerned. Show me how to experience Your grace to the fullest. Help me to show that same kind of grace to those around me."

"There is therefore now no condemnation to those who are in Christ Jesus, who do not walk according to the flesh, but according to the Spirit. For the law of the Spirit of life in Christ Jesus has made me free from the law of sin and death."

Romans 8:1-2

"For all the law is fulfilled in one word, even in this: "You shall love your neighbor as yourself."

Galatians 5:14

"But if you are led by the Spirit, you are not under the law."

Galatians 5:18

RESOURCES:

- *Pure Grace* by Clark Whitten
- *Unfiltered Grace by* Joe Langley
- *Beyond an Angry God* by Steve McVey

Developing a Healthy "Giving" Culture

"Give, and it'll be given unto you; good measure, pressed down, shaken together and running over will be put in your bosom. For with the same measure you use, it will be measured back to you" (Luke 6:38).
—Jesus

Money has the potential to be a controversial topic, but for Kingdom people, it shouldn't be. A clear understanding of tithes and offerings is definitely one of *The Best Kept Secrets In The Kingdom*. I have found that most people in the church today, as well as many of its leaders, don't have a solid Biblical handle on the teaching of tithes and offerings. Most are satisfied to just stick with the 10% rule and leave it at that. Even though statistics tell us that Christians nowadays only give an average of about 2.5% of their total income which, incidentally is nearly a full percentage point below what they were giving during the Great Depression, most are still confused about how, and how much to give. If a healthy culture of giving is to be established in any church, there must be clear Biblical teaching on the subject.

Because money is such an important issue affecting every person in every area of society, it makes sense for Kingdom people to take a closer look so we can come away with a sensible mindset to know how we should handle our finances and to know how to give to churches and ministries in a Biblical way. Since the "freewill" giving of tithes and offerings is the only Biblical means of support for the church, its "employees," (both ministry and support positions) all its programs and activities, including evangelism and missions, it's vital that it is communicated in a clear and concise way as to help every person, along with the help of the Holy Spirit, to know what to do. Doing so guarantees the individual and the church to be blessed in incredible ways.

The first mention of the tithe in the Bible is found in Genesis 12. Abraham had returned from war and gave a tenth (tithe) of all he had to Melchizedek, the King of Salem. I think it's important to notice that in the wars Abraham was engaged in, and won, he couldn't help but notice that he'd won them "only" because God helped him! In this way, he was acknowledging and bringing the due honor to God. If one looks closely, you can find the principle of the tithe and offering much earlier in scripture. Cain and Abel brought their offerings to the Lord. Cain brought an offering of the fruit of the ground, but Abel brought of the firstlings (tithe) of the flock and of the "fat" (offering), thereof. Although there is no mention of it up to that point, it seems clear that Adam and Eve had taught their boys something about worship, and subsequently about giving.

As you know, Abel's offering was acceptable to God. He brought what was required, but he also, in giving of the fat thereof, gave more than what was required. His gift was a clear indicator of the condition of his heart. In Biblical days the giving of the tithe and offering wasn't so much in money or legal tender of some kind but in animals, crops, new wine, or other possessions. There were clear instructions in the Levitical Law as to how individuals should prepare to give. It was a requirement of the Law. However, for those who argue that the tithe is an Old Covenant principle, it's important to bear in mind that Abraham's tithe to Melchizedek came 430 years before the Law was instituted with the nation of Israel.

Since the Levites, the tribe responsible for all the ministry around the tabernacle, had no inheritance in the Promised Land, the tithe was brought to the "storehouse." It was used by the Levites for their sustenance and livelihood. The other eleven tribes had a parcel of land where they could plant crops, raise livestock, and make a living, but not the Levites. This Old Testament pattern is symbolic (a type and shadow) of those called into full-time ministry in modern times. "Those who preach the gospel should live from the gospel." That 10% was solely for the Levites and for ministry to the poor. With very little exception, none of the tithe was used for anything other than that. Some would even say that tithing is not "giving." I agree. In reality, tithing is just rendering to God that which is already His. While that may be true, communicating it as such could be very offensive to those just starting to get obedient in their giving. A willful tithe is a 10% confession that everything belongs to God.

The Levites were also required to tithe. However, the Levites tithe was specifically designated to Aaron (The High Priest) and his four sons, symbolic of the fivefold ministries today. Some churches as well as some leaders may choose to give a tithe of the tithe to outside ministries they have chosen to relate to. These fivefold ministries are often given authority by local church leaders where counsel, oversight, and accountability are concerned. The tithe of the tithe provides compensation for those apostolic ministries (See in Church Government: Spheres of Authority).

Most ministry leaders, when teaching on the tithe and offering start their teaching from Malachi 3. "Will a man rob God?" There's a great lesson to be found there, and blessings to be had, no doubt. The mistake is often made to leave God's people under condemnation if they're not giving their 10%. Much of the population of the Body of Christ give because they believe they're going to be under a curse if they don't. While that may have been the case under the Law, it's not good teaching from that position now that we're under grace and no longer under the Old Covenant of Law.

Malachi was issuing a charge against the people of God, more specifically the priests, in his generation. Speaking on God's behalf, he declared they had robbed God in tithes and offerings. The word tithe simply means 10%; nothing more, nothing less. Offerings are anything that's over and above the tithe. Most in the modern church are so serious about their checkbook that even talk about 10% makes them nervous, and any mention of more than that can cause some serious emotional stress. Of course, it's wise to be frugal and a good steward, so how the tithe and offering is communicated becomes an extremely important task.

To get to the bottom of the Truth found in Malachi 3, one must look at it from a New Covenant perspective. While we're not under the legalistic requirement of the Old Covenant as it relates to giving tithes and offerings in Malachi's day, we may be able to receive the blessings recorded there. Looking at Malachi 3 through the New Covenant lens changes everything. What if, with our new perspective, we understood (began to see) that it was now no longer a requirement but rather an invitation? That changes everything and reconciles Malachi's words with the New Covenant. Let's look at the blessings recorded in Malachi 3. The blessings:

> *Try me now, in this,"* says the Lord:
> - *If I will not open the windows of heaven*
> - *Pour you out a blessing you won't have room enough to receive.*
> - *Rebuke the devourer for your sakes*
> - *He will not destroy the fruit of your ground*
> - *Your vine will not cast it's fruit in the field before its time*
> - *All nations will call you blessed*
> - *You will be a delightful land*

As others have observed, this is the only time in the entire Bible that God issues a challenge such as this; "Try me now in this …," says the Lord. While this was written generations ago we can get a clear glimpse into how the Lord wants to respond to our obedience in giving. He is asking us to put Him to the test in our giving and His promise is to bless us in a magnitude of ways. I've heard it said that the tithe opens the windows of heaven, and the offering regulates the flow of resources from God. I like that description.

I would define the "storehouse" in modern times as the place where you are being fed and equipped, more specifically, the church which you are led to be a part of. That being said, the tithe would serve to bless the minister(s) and ministry at that particular church. When thinking about the offering, that which is over and above the tithe, there are two issues to be considered. First, you should be made aware of the known needs of the church such as building funds, missions, youth projects, etc. As you know these needs you may feel impressed by the Lord to give toward those. Secondly, there's what I call giving by revelation. It's exciting to put out a plea to the Lord as to who, what, where, and how much He might direct you to give. I've heard many incredible stories from those who are willing to give by revelation and have experienced the blessing myself. It's also interesting to note that in Old Testament times on more than one occasion when there was a temple or tabernacle to be constructed, the tithe was never used for those things. Instead, a plea was put out in the kingdom for people to bring their freewill offerings. They did so to such a degree that finally, they were told to stop their giving. They had received too much!! The kingdom law of sowing and reaping can't help but work when we decide to give it a try.

There must be a healthy balance in the church in teaching on giving. Leaders may often feel that if they teach on giving that they will be perceived as being "all about money." I understand that feeling well, but in all actuality, what we're doing as leaders is throwing a "life raft" to our people where their finances are concerned. A healthy balance in teaching on giving would prohibit overemphasizing, manipulation, coercion and in some extreme cases, flat out condemnation. That's not the Kingdom way! It's the leader's responsibility to educate and impart a healthy culture of giving by teaching Biblical principles to his people. When that's done, the whole Body is able to prosper and to experience the supernatural blessing of the Lord.

Giving Activates the Supernatural Realm

I grew up on a ranch in the Texas Panhandle. Although we believed in God, we didn't go to church. I remember, every year, my Dad would give the preacher in the little town of Allison, Texas beef. We were in the cattle business. We would sort off, feed and fatten a few calves every year and get them to the slaughterhouse for our own use and sometimes sell some of the beef as well. But we always gave the preacher some, too. In my uneducated mind, I thought, "Heck, we're good with God." I didn't know any better at the time. I can look back now, and it seems clear that the Lord, somehow, blessed us because of it. When I started going to church at age 30, I had no reference point as to how much I should give. In fact, I was so ignorant about Biblical giving that I thought if I put a $20 bill in the offering plate that I was kind of doing the Lord a favor—sad, and extremely immature, but true for where I was at the time.

It wasn't long before we started to learn about the tithe and offering. We immediately decided it was the right thing to do, to start tithing. We were living paycheck to paycheck, but still, we made the commitment to tithe. An interesting phenomenon presented itself. When we sat down to pay our bills and figured how much our tithe should be it was apparent that we wouldn't have enough left to give that much. Determined to do right by the Lord anyway we started at that point writing that tithe check first. It is, after all as we learned, a "firstfruits" offering. The most amazing thing happened. Now, when we paid our bills we miraculously had enough! That was when I learned that giving activates the supernatural realm. Something happens when we get obedient in our personal giving.

We then caught the revelation of giving offerings; that which is over and above the tithe. Again, we had no idea how we were going to do it. We just knew we should. One particular month we had tithed, our bills were paid and I sat at my table and said to the Lord, "I want to give an offering. What do I need to do?" Immediately the name of a personal friend in another state came to mind and just as quickly I heard a specific amount. It was an odd amount, $80. I wrote the check, drove the three miles to my mailbox and put the letter in the mail. I didn't see this friend for several months but when I did see him he broke into tears and said, "That money you sent me, it was the exact amount we had to have, and it came on the exact day we had to have it!" That day the verse that says, "It's more blessed to give than to receive" became very real to me! I'll say it again, "When we get obedient in our giving, something supernatural happens!"

A few weeks later, during a Sunday morning service, I glanced over to see Julie writing a check to another family in our church who were going through a rough time. I looked at the check amount and immediately thought, "We don't have that much in our account!" We were testing our faith, and I totally trust Julie's ability to hear the Lord. Now, to rewind a couple of weeks. I trained horses for clients during that time. A person from two hours away called me and asked my price to train three horses for him. I gave him my price, and he said, "I really want you to do it. I just can't afford it." That was the end of the conversation. I was understandably a little sad because we really needed the money. Now, back to that Sunday in church. We went home to the ranch for the afternoon and then back for the Sunday night service. Julie gave the check to the family after church and home we went. When we opened the door of our house the phone rang. It was the man with the three horses. He said, "I'm bringing all three horses tomorrow!" I knew that was directly connected to the check Julie gave our friends. The income from those three horses was over ten times the amount of the check Julie gave our friends.

Conclusion

One of the easiest and most understandable methods in teaching Biblical giving is to focus on the law of sowing and reaping. It doesn't get any simpler than that. If a farmer wants to reap a bumper crop of wheat, he can't be skimpy at planting time. Obviously, the more seed he plants the more he will reap at harvest time. "As a man sows, so shall he reap."

> *"For God so loved the world He gave His Only Begotten Son, that whoever believes in Him should not perish but have everlasting life."*
> John 3:16

God's love is expressed by 'giving'! It's a fundamental character trait of the Father. It should also be a fundamental trait of His children! As we grow in our relationship with the Father and develop a healthy Kingdom mindset as it relates to giving our minds are transformed from, thinking we have to or need to give, to actually wanting to give!

It makes good spiritual sense to learn the Biblical criteria for giving. You and your church will blessed as a result. If we'll do that, and be consistent, a healthy giving culture will be produced. Then, we can then move this one off the list of *The Best Kept Secrets In The Kingdom*.

Quit Telling Me What the Problem Is!

It was a bit of a rude awakening when we were informed that the ranch we had leased, lived on for nearly 25 years, made our homes, and were assured we'd be there forever, was going to be sold. I'll never forget that day! Interestingly enough, the day before, I had written inside the cover of my Bible: "God, I want everything You have for me, no matter what it costs me." I had no idea that the very next day, He would begin to shift things in such a way that I could clearly see, at least a little of what the "costs" might be! It was, even more, the challenge because Julie and I had absolutely no back-up plan. As far as we were concerned, we were going to raise our kids and grow old there. So everything was somewhat in chaos, and we had no choice but to put our trust in the Lord.

That was in 1988, and we moved only 30 miles away south of Cheyenne, Oklahoma. I worked several odd jobs for a few months, everything from helping take care of cattle (which I was way familiar with), to some oilfield day work but nothing extremely stable or permanent. I saw an ad in the local paper and went for an interview, took an aptitude test and was hired on the spot by Edgar Sellers (before he even looked at how I'd done on the test), a great guy who'd be my boss for the next seven years. I started with Western Merchandisers the next week!

The president of the company was John Marmaduke, whose dad, Sam, had started the company on a shoestring a generation before. John was a brilliant businessman, in my opinion. He took a fairly small company and procured a contract with Wal-Mart that eventually enabled Western Merchandisers to supply all the music (vinyl, LP's, 8-Tracks, Cassettes, CDs), the books, all the computer software, and most of the movies for the entire Wal-Mart chain, nationwide. After a few years, Wal-Mart purchased Western Merchandisers for millions.

John was an aggressive guy in our regional meetings. He knew the business and didn't tolerate amateurism to any degree. Let's just say he 'ran a tight ship'! I remember several meetings with sales reps, district managers, and upper-level management when people would start to talk of all the problems out in the field. John would rip into them—no matter what level they were. I can remember him saying more than a few times, "I'm tired of hearing about the problems; Anybody can tell you what the problems are!", "I want to hear from somebody who has a solution!"

I've never forgotten those meetings and what I learned from John. And, it's true; whether we're talking about the Federal Government, the Little League Baseball Team, the Chamber for Commerce, your marriage or the Church; just about anybody can tell you what the problem is. You don't have to be genius to figure that out! There's just not many out there who are solution minded.

So, quit telling me what the problem is! I want to hear from somebody who has a solution!

> This and more thoughts from Andy can be found at his blog:
> *"The Way I See It"* - www.andyrtaylor.com.

PLAN OF ACTION:

- Do some further study on the tithe and offering and begin to move in obedience to what you learn
- Commit to be a faithful giver
- Find out the needs in your church so you can pray and plan how to give offerings
- Pray that the Lord would direct you in the giving of offerings
- Learn to give by revelation

LEADERS:

- Develop a solid Scriptural teaching on giving
- Do not avoid teaching on giving
- Teach the difference between the tithe and the offering
- Understand that you are helping your people
- Teach periodically on giving as to keep your people informed and motivated

PRAY:

"Father, help me to understand Your perfect pattern for giving. Help me to give systematically and by revelation."

Tithers make up only 10-25 percent of a normal congregation. Churches that accept tithing online increase overall donations by 32%. Only 5% tithe and 80% of Americans only give 2% of their income. Christians are giving at 2.5% of income; during the Great Depression, it was 3.3%.

Embracing Destiny

"For I know the plans I have for you, plans to prosper you
and not to harm you, plans to give you hope and a future" (Jeremiah 29:11).
—God

There is a deep awareness inside us that God has a plan for our life. That awareness has been imparted to us from the Father. But the challenges life throws at us have a unique way of diverting us and maybe even derailing us away from that plan if we're not careful. Embracing destiny is vital if we're to fulfill the plan God has for each of us. In my experience of leading people, I've observed that many, if not most, people either don't have a sense of destiny or have lost sight of it. Whatever the reason, and considering the results one might produce who understands their destiny, it easily earns its right to be included among *The Best Kept Secrets In The Kingdom*.

> *"For you formed my inward parts; You covered me in my mother's womb. I will praise You, for I am fearfully and wonderfully made; Marvelous are Your works, and that my soul knows very well. My frame was not hidden from You when I was made in secret and skillfully wrought in the lowest parts of the earth. Your eyes saw my substance, being yet unformed. And in Your book they all were written, the days fashioned for me when as yet there were none of them."*
> Psalm 139:13-16

That's a beautiful passage of Scripture. The truth exposed and the ramifications for each of us is even more intriguing. Before we were created God had already written down the "sum of our days." That's some kind of advance planning! The writer of that psalm talks of a "book" where the details of our life are recorded. The book referred to is not the Bible since the specifics of each of our lives are NOT written there. It's obvious to me why the Father didn't record those things in the Bible. If we had access to all those things in some kind of document we wouldn't have any reason to go to Him for the secrets of our lives. For me, this passage is clearly an invitation to come closer to Him in relationship, interact with Him and let Him tell us the things that are in His heart for us. It seems important to mention here that as important as the Bible is, it's not a substitute for our relationship with the Father. In fact, the Bible has been written and compiled in such a way as to lead us to an encounter with Him. That's what the Father wants! That's what our lives are all about.

Destiny:
The events that will necessarily happen to a particular person or thing in the future; the hidden power believed to control what will happen in the future; fate.

I talk a lot about destiny. I think it's extremely important. As we draw closer to the Father, He gives us glimpses into our destiny. Everything He does, and the things He says to us serves to pull us (He doesn't push!) into a deeper level of faith; those things always lead us in the direction of our destiny. When people hear us talk about destiny, some might think we're talking about destination. That's not the case at all. If you're born again, your destination, which is Heaven, is already settled. Destiny includes all the events and all the people along the way to your destination. Our destiny always includes people. When I think about my own destiny, I think of how, at age 30, I wasn't at all on the path of my destiny, as I now understand it. My encounter with the Father dramatically corrected my course! When I talk about my destiny with our church, I always tell them that each of them have now become a critical and important part of my own destiny. Now, I don't think so highly of myself to think if I hadn't answered the call of God on my life that all these people who are now part of my life would've somehow gotten lost in the shuffle. God is good enough at what He does that He wouldn't allow that to happen. I do believe that when I said, "Yes" to His plan, they all became part of my destiny. In retrospect, I can't imagine what my life might have been like without this incredible family of people to live with.

Having a sense of destiny can be a very powerful component in the life of any believer. The inner witness of the Spirit helps us in a variety of ways. When a person becomes aware of their destiny, passion is ignited. It's a natural by-product! An awareness of destiny is a strong motivator in life whenever we get knocked down or discouraged. The Holy Spirit is so good to encourage us during those times. He helps us to realize this is not the end; this set of problems is not going to get the best of us; if we feel stalled out, we know this is not the end of our journey; the glory of God is in front of us! With a sense of destiny, we're prone to get back up and get back in the game, oftentimes with a new zeal and greater focus to pursue our destiny. Having a sense of destiny is simply understanding that God really does have a plan for our life, and then starting to walk in that direction.

It grieves me to think about those who might not be aware of their destiny or those who have lost sight of it. I think it's the second worse thing that could possibly happen to us in our lifetime. Of course, the worse thing would be to miss our appointment with salvation. Missing the main reason we exist would be an epic "miss," indeed! It would be a sad thing to gain the whole world and lose your life (the reason for your existence) in the process.

Stop and think about it; God has called you to greatness. It makes sense to find out the details of your life from Him. You'll enjoy Him, and the process, as well as the satisfaction of fulfilling your destiny!

It's Not Too Late to Make a "Mark" With Your Life!

We're all born with an inherent need to make a difference with our life. There is something resident deep down inside us that makes us want our lives to "count." I believe it's the work of the Lord, without a doubt. Not many people would argue that the Father has an intricate, detailed plan for their life. When it comes right down to it, many of those same people would be hard-pressed to confess that His plan was being adequately worked out in their life at the moment.

Well, I, for one, think we need to think about doing something about that. Fulfilling our destiny is a serious thing to consider. The worst thing that could happen to us in our lifetime is to ignore or reject the Holy spirit's attempts to draw us to the Lord. For us to miss salvation would be a tragedy almost beyond comprehension. To miss our destiny (the God-ordained plan He has for our life) would be the "second" worst thing that could happen to us. To be on the planet for our allotted time and miss the reason why we exist would be a "miss" of epic proportions! There's no sense in letting that happen.

If you're going to fulfill your destiny and make a mark with your life, I wouldn't piddle around too long, 'cause the clock's ticking. Here's what to do:

1) Renew your relationship with the Father.
2) Communicate with Him; Talk to him, listen, be aware of how He wants to move in your life.
3) Be obedient; It's going to take faith for you to proceed. The good news is, you already have adequate faith!
4) Commit to the long-haul. * It's a lifelong endeavor!
5) Expect some obstacles; There'll be plenty, but you're an overcomer.

> 6) Pay close attention to the people in your path; they're a "key" to your destiny!
> 7) Enjoy the trip!
>   It's not too late to make a mark with your life!
>
> *This and more thoughts from Andy can be found at his blog: "The Way I See It" - www.andyrtaylor.com.*

PLAN OF ACTION:

- Start now being aware that God has a plan for you
- Take note of the things God shows you about your life
- Use your faith to move in the direction of your destiny
- Be sensitive to the Holy Spirit as He leads you in the direction of your destiny
- Learn to see every event as an important facet of your destiny
- Be aware of the people the Father brings into your life

LEADERS:

- Develop and nurture your own sense of destiny
- Teach your people the importance of destiny
- Help your people in practical ways to fulfill their destiny

PRAY:

"Father, thank You that You have meticulously planned out my life. Help me to see and be aware of the glimpses You give of my destiny. Help me to get on track with Your plan for my life."

Shaping An Agape Culture

"And now abide faith, hope and love, these three; but the greatest of these is love" (1 Cor. 13:13).
—Jesus

I grew up in a household where the "I love you's" were very common. I didn't realize how important that was until I was all grown up. As a matter of fact, I don't guess I really came to the stark realization of just how important that was until I began to encounter person after person who didn't have the same luxury as me. It has been a bit of an eye-opener of how many people my age never heard their dad say, "I love you." From experience, I'd say that moms are traditionally a lot better to say it than dads. Saying it is important—more important than you might imagine.

In my part of the world (I've been in the Texas Panhandle or Western Oklahoma all my life), it seems to have been part of the culture. Not sure if the same would go for other parts of the USA or the rest of the world for that matter, but it wouldn't surprise me. The fact is there are myriads of people out there who didn't hear "I love you" in their home, from their parents or their people and as a result, they don't say it either. It makes an incredible difference to hear it. I can't number the times I've sat in my office with people of all ages with one after the other recanting their heartbreak over wondering if they were loved at all. Of course, in most, if not nearly all cases, they were loved, just not told.

I'm free with the term, and I've found out that if you tell other people you love 'em in a little bit, they'll return the favor. For many who are not free with it, it may feel very awkward and unnatural at first, but as time goes by, it'll start to feel like second-nature. My best example is one of my close friends, Buddy Suthers; he grew up in one of those homes where he was loved, but it just wasn't said. He caught the significance of what I'm talking about and started the process with his grown sons. It caught on! Now I'll walk through our offices and hear him on the phone with one of his boys, and they'll finish the call with, "Love Ya." It blesses me to hear that! It's doable, and you can do it too!

If we have a mind to do it, let's learn to love everyone like He does.

It's one of the most significant stories in the New Testament, the Gentiles being brought into the family of God. It was unheard of. For the Jews, it was outright blasphemy. It had been prophesied generations before, but it becomes a reality in Acts chapter 10. There is some powerful truth contained in this story, and if the twenty-first-century church can grasp it, it'll be revolutionary at the very least! The issue at the center of this critical chapter is whether or not we can love the people the Father loves, and whether or not we can love them like He loves them. His love is not superficial, it's not based on our behavior or our performance. Now, don't get me wrong; He definitely wants our behavior to change for the better. He loves it when we're obedient to Him by faith in the circumstances of life. After all, He wants to conform us into the image of His Son. But His love was given to us before we could do anything to earn it. In fact, His Word says, "God demonstrates His love toward us in that Jesus died for us while we were still sinners." The issue is this; can we love those people and people groups that seem to be so separated from God, those that are thoroughly engaged in a sinful lifestyle? Religion and the religious mind would quickly say no. But not the Father! No, His love is unconditional and without limits. He loves the Buddhist as well as the adulterer, the atheist, and the hypocrite alike. And that quality of immeasurable love gives the sinner a chance to change. Until we, in the church, can love like the Father loves, we're stuck in a lifeless organization that's not much like Him.

Now, here's something serious to think about. If we didn't hear "I love you" from our parents and if we truly believe we weren't loved, when we start to connect with God, who is a Father, it's conceivable that He couldn't love us either. While that's the farthest thing from the truth you'd be surprised how many people actually believe it. It profoundly affects the most important relationship you'll ever have! The more you trust the Father, the more fulfilling your life will be! We need to fix this! In the end, we all want to hear, "Well, done good and faithful servant." What if it comes down to this "one thing?" Did we love like he loves? Love never fails; it's undefeated!

Here's my proposition: I'm starting an "I love you" culture! It might even turn into a revolution. Wouldn't that be something? Who's with me?

If You Love Someone, You Should Tell Them!

I've had the amazing good fortune to have grown up in a household where the term, "I love you," was a very regular happening. Cliff and Charlene Taylor never let an opportunity to say it, go by. I think I'd be safe in saying that Monty (my brother) and I heard "I love you" most every day of our young lives. I've never had to go a single day in my 67 years, wondering if I was loved by them. They're now in their '80's and live just a few blocks from me. I see them several times a week and talk to them on the phone almost every day, and every single time, without exception, we tell one another, "I love you"! I think it makes a difference.

We have a 'built-in' need to be loved, and hearing it from those around us goes a long way in meeting that need. Of course, to say it and not show it with our actions doesn't do much good. It needs to be both! I can't tell you how many times I've listened in my office to men and women, some younger, some older than me, who agonize over the fact that their dad never told them that he loved them. I don't think I've ever heard even one of them say that their mom never told them that she loved them. Maybe moms are better at it; maybe it's the validation of a father that we so desperately need. In most cases, it isn't that the dad didn't love them; it's that they weren't told that themselves. In our culture, as wrong as it may be, men saying, "I love you," just isn't cool.

I'm on a lifelong crusade to encourage you, whoever you are, to tell the people in your life that you love them! I've seen quite a few that didn't grow up in an "I love you" culture who have broken the pattern. It has changed everything for the better. They all agree! If you love someone, by all means, show them by your actions. But don't forget to tell them too!

This and more thoughts from Andy can be found at his blog:
"The Way I See It" - www.andyrtaylor.com.

Displacing the Religious Spirit

*"You have made the commandment of God
of no effect by your tradition" (Matthew 15:6).*
—Jesus

Jesus came to challenge, and ultimately displace, the religious spirit that existed in His time. The culture was entrenched in the Jewish Law, and its adherents were unwilling to budge. But Jesus was on a mission. One that His Father had specifically set in motion. Even though all the forces of hell were deployed against Him, He would not be deterred! Because of the challenges involved and the fact that only a few are willing to go against the demonic spirit of religion, it must be included in *The Best Kept Secrets In The Kingdom.*

Any of the principles addressed in this book if adhered to (... and why wouldn't you?) will cause you to go against the grain of normalized, and in many cases, dead religion. Introducing a newer, better, or more effective way of doing things in the church sounds like a great idea. When it comes to implementing those things in an environment where religious tradition has a strong foothold, it's a monumental undertaking. The old saying is true, "Many have tried; many have died!" The gauntlet has been thrown down. As Kingdom people, we have the responsibility, along with the authority and power needed to respond valiantly to the challenge!

"What's wrong with religious tradition," you might ask? Well, nothing. Nothing that is, unless that tradition is keeping the Kingdom of God from being established and advanced, and keeping you from being who you're supposed to be. In that case, religious tradition is not just a bad thing; it's the most evil thing. It was the most evil thing in Jesus' time on earth. He bumped up against it numerous times every single day. You will, likewise, go up against it following the will of the Father and in the pursuit of your destiny! You might as well get used to it.

Someone once said, "Tradition always dies screaming!" I totally agree. Except when it's religious tradition we're talking about, it's even more true. When we started here in 1989, the little group of people had all kinds of great ideas on what we needed to do to build a successful church. They were right-hearted, no doubt about it. All their ideas were derived from the religious environment they had previously been a part of. There were some from the Church of Christ, Methodist, Baptist, Pentecostal and

Charismatic churches. As you can imagine there was a menagerie of great ideas of what we should do. I was green as a gourd. Heck, I had only even been in church consistently for less than five years. One thing I knew; Jesus is the Builder of the church. Even though I loved this little band of people I knew I couldn't bend and crumble under their demands. It was hard; very good for me, but really, really hard. God doesn't mind the "man" of God being between a rock and a hard place. Well, in this instance it would be between The Rock and a hard place! It is a test of epic proportions for anyone He's shaping to be a Kingdom leader. God needs to know if His leaders are going to be persuaded by people, or influenced and led by Him! I had to tell the people, "I don't have the liberty to build this church my way." "I sure don't have the liberty to build it your way!" If it's going to work at all it has to be done His way! "Unless the Lord builds the house, they labor in vain who build it" (Psalms 127:1).

A great type and shadow of this subject are found in the Old Testament when God gave instructions on the building of the tabernacle in the wilderness. One particular Sunday, as I was teaching, I talked about the tabernacle. As you know, it wasn't a permanent structure. It was built like it was so it could be portable. When the cloud by day or the pillar of fire by night moved, the tabernacle moved with it. As I taught, I said, "It was just a tent." While that was true when I said that the Lord quietly but deliberately said to my spirit, "Andy, it wasn't JUST a tent!" I got the point. When I went to the Word and checked it out, I found there were in the neighborhood of 250 verses, specifically detailing how the tabernacle was to be built. So, yes, it was a tent; but it wasn't "just" a tent! The point I want to make here is this: the Lord had specific instructions for every little facet of the tabernacle. After it was finished and everything was done according to God's pattern, the glory of God filled the tabernacle! I strongly believe if any of the persons working on that tabernacle had decided to do it another way or decided that some other material should be used other than what the Lord prescribed, the Israelites would've never experienced God's glory. The lesson here: If we build according to His' pattern," we can expect the glory of God. That should cause us to wonder what changes or adjustments need to be made in the church today so we can experience like the Israelites did, the glory of God.

Mainstream Religion

Years ago, I heard from the Lord, "Andy, what I'm doing here is not mainstream. But I want it to be." I immediately knew that to be the voice of God. It had that familiar feel. When I thought about it, I saw that it was the same with Jesus when He came to the earth. Jesus didn't represent the status quo. Nor did He adapt to the world's expressions of religion. He was on a mission from Heaven to establish an unshakable Kingdom, one marked with supernatural power, life, and unconditional love. Just like the Lord spoke to me, what Jesus was sent to do was not mainstream, but God wanted it to be! It has always behooved me when someone comes to my church from a dead church (by their own assessment) and, in six months, be mad at me because I'm not doing things like they were. Again, that's religious tradition at its finest.

"We Don't Do That Stuff Here"

I love John Wimber's story. A professional musician with virtually no spiritual foundation, he was responsible for pairing the Righteous Brothers together in the 60s, and the duo became known worldwide. While performing in Las Vegas, he would drive out into the desert late at night, wondering if there was more to life. Little did he know that it was God causing the feeling that something was missing in his life. Fast forward, John did get gloriously saved, came under the mentorship of a man by the name of Gunnar Payne. Payne taught Wimber about Jesus. He learned of the miracles, signs, and wonders Jesus performed. Payne taught John that those things could be part of our lives as well. With a childlike heart, John just believed those things. After attending a church for a time, he said to a friend after a night service, "When are we gonna do the stuff?" His friend asked, "What stuff?" "You know, healing the sick, casting out demons." "That kind of stuff." His friend gave him a disgusting look and quickly said, "Uh, we don't do that stuff here." It's a sad but true commentary on much of the church today. Just like Jesus said, "Because of your tradition, you have made the commandments of God of no effect." Oh, incidentally, John Wimber later became head of the Vineyard movement worldwide. The Vineyard Church, with over 2400 churches around the world, became known for its heartfelt, extravagant worship and where miracles of all kinds became commonplace. Let's agree together to contend for that kind of power to be displayed by the church in our generation!

As your devotion and commitment to the Lord grow, you'll be accosted by the religious spirit. As the old saying goes, "It's not 'if' it'll happen, it's 'when.'" It's a guarantee. The religious spirit can be a very vicious and distracting thing to deal with. More often than not, it will come through people you know and love. Religious people, those going through the motions and not in relation with God, are some of the meanest people in the world. They know how to be vicious and vindictive. They'll fight to the death for their religious tradition, even though much of it's dead in the water! Going through many of those battles through the years caused me to come to this conclusion; "Kingdom people will die for what they believe; religious people will kill for what they believe." It's at this point you'll need to remember, "we wrestle not against flesh and blood, but against principalities, powers and the spiritual host of wickedness in heavenly places!" It's a spiritual battle of epic proportions and one that, if fought exclusively in the flesh, you could find yourself on the losing end, at least temporarily. There will also be times you will feel like you're trying to swim upstream. Because of my own experiences, I would go a step farther to say, "You might even feel like you're trying to swim up a waterfall!" It's all worth it to see the Kingdom of God established and the true church taking shape with the supernatural ability to change the world.

It's a high-call, perilous and dangerous, indeed. If you're up to it, and if we can get the masses to buy-in, we can eventually displace the religious spirit with a Kingdom spirit. Then we can remove it from the list of *The Best Kept Secrets In The Kingdom*.

How Gunner Payne Changed the World

You've heard of Gunner Payne, right? Just kidding, I'd be willing to bet the whole ranch that you've never heard of him. Gunner Payne changed the world in an extremely profound way. Gunner was a Quaker. You may have heard of the Quakers, but if you're like me, you don't know much about them.

Gunner had a regular Bible study, in the early 60s, in his hometown of Yorba Linda, California. In '62, Dick Heying, a professional drummer, took his bandleader and his wife to Gunner's Bible study. Not too long after that (early '63), both were saved. They became very faithful as Gunner took them 'under his wing' as a mentor and father in the Lord. It wasn't long before John and Carol were winning people to the Lord themselves. John, a professional musician, was the person who put The Righteous Brothers together. Over the next few years, hundreds came to know Jesus in a personal way. John later said that he just mimicked Gunner's behavior and attitude.

Gunner's life wasn't without major obstacles; his little 4-year-old daughter was kidnapped by a migrant farmworker from a neighboring community who raped and murdered her. The incident brought about a lot of national media attention that went on for months. It was a tragedy of epic proportions. The fascinating part of the story is what happened next; Gunner Payne went to the prison where the murderer was incarcerated at least once a month until he finally won his little girl's killer to the Lord!

Remember John and Carol? They are the Wimbers. While John Wimber didn't initiate the Vineyard Movement, he's the one that the Lord used to bring it to worldwide prominence and influence. (Now over 1500 churches worldwide) If you're in church today and not singing from a denominational hymnal, you're singing songs directly influenced by Wimber and the Vineyard Movement. It brought a whole new style of worship to the forefront, worldwide, and spawned great worship leaders across the globe. John was a huge proponent of "signs and wonders;" his ministry was marked with miracles of every kind. Hundreds of thousands have come to know the Lord because of the ministry of John Wimber.

You just never know what might happen with the people that you're willing to invest in!

That's how Gunner Payne changed the world!

Good job, Gunner!

This and more thoughts from Andy can be found at his blog: "The Way I See It" - www.andyrtaylor.com.

PLAN OF ACTION:

- Have a strong resolve to be obedient to the Father
- Do the things He tells you to do
- Stay under authority in your church
- Stay humble
- Guard your own heart
- Watch out for pride!

LEADERS:

- As the Lord reveals changes that need to happen, be obedient
- SLOW DOWN! Kingdom change must happen slowly but deliberately
- If you will do this, you will minimize casualties
- Don't be intimidated by the religious spirit
- Stay on the mission of having a Kingdom church
- Remember: It's a lifetime endeavor

PRAY:

"Father, help me to be a Kingdom person. Help me to have a heart for the things You're doing. Help me to shake off useless tradition. Help me to recognize and deal with the spirit of religion."

Conclusion

If The Church is Going to be The Church

*"On this rock I will build My church,
and the gates of Hell shall not prevail against it"* (Matt. 16:18).
—Jesus

If the church is going to be the church we see depicted in the Bible; the glorious and powerful organism filled with the love of God, these are things that must happen:

- Knowing about God must give way to actually knowing Him
- Prayer as an option must give way to prayer as a necessity and the incredible opportunity to communicate with the Father that it is
- Well constructed sermons must give way to the Word of God being declared
- Song services must give way to true worship done in spirit and truth
- Holding ground and maintaining a position must give way to advancing the Kingdom of God
- People inactive and sitting on the sidelines must give way to the entire family of God being equipped for the work of the ministry
- Talking about faith must give way to walking by faith
- Grace argued about must give way to a deeper understanding of grace and genuine grace expressed
- Believing IN signs and wonders must give way to believing FOR signs and wonders
- Talking about miracles must give way to contending for and operating in miracles
- Superficial relationships must give way to deep sovereign God-arranged relationships
- The term "church family" must give way to a genuine expression of the Family of God
- The religious status quo must give way to the ongoing manifestation of the Kingdom of God
- Love talked about must give way to Agape expressed!

- You, as just another insignificant Christian that doesn't make a difference in the world, must give way to the new creation you are and awakening to the incredible destiny God has designed for you.

We stand on the brink of the greatest move of God the world will ever see. We have been strategically positioned by the Father, Himself. We are each gifted and equipped in supernatural ways to be powerfully effective in everything we do. This is our time!

"If It Ain't Broke, Break It!"

I've always been a reader. Down through the years, I've read books of all kinds and enjoyed most of them. These days I don't mess around with a book too much; if it doesn't capture me in the first 10-15 pages, I'm putting it down. Most books I've bought, I at least had some kind of an idea what they were about before I laid the cash down. But I bought a book 25 or so years ago by the above title, "If It Ain't Broke, Break It!" It turns out, it was a life-changer for me. I couldn't have known how much, going in, but looking back, it shaped me in some good ways.

The title was 'catchy', you gotta admit that! The statement totally goes against conventional thinking and logic, right? It's not a spiritual book, although many of the principles have found their way into what I've been doing the past 32 years. It's more of a business book. Logic, even common sense, would say, "If it ain't broke, don't fix it." But this book is based on the idea/assumption that businesses that at one time had a lion's share of the market in their particular field somehow got lazy and complacent and then began to lose their footing. It happened with Xerox, IBM, Levis, and other well-known brands. They were the "Big Dogs," so to speak....but their lackadaisical attitude allowed much smaller, hungry little upstart companies to steal away much of their business. And to this day they've never fully regained it.

Where it has helped me, in what I do as a church leader, is not to get complacent and lazy. I don't feel that I have to reinvent the wheel, but I do know that I need to stay relevant for the generation. If I'm going to do that, I need to look at what I'm saying and doing periodically and then be honest with myself when it starts to feel stale.

The church in America is in a quandary. I hesitate to say that it's broken, but it is definitely gasping for air. What used to work doesn't seem to work anymore. Conventional thinking and common sense have flatlined. And the 'organism' that should be exuding life to our culture has turned into an organization. We're behind the curve of the twenty-first century. Every other thing is moving along at warp speed, but the church seems to just be plodding along, wondering why everyone's not jumping on board.

You may not agree, and that's OK with me. But maybe, just maybe we need to look at where we're at and take the book's advice!

This and more thoughts from Andy can be found at his blog: "The Way I See It" - www.andyrtaylor.com.

Who is God?

"God is What He is; Father is Who He Is"
—AT

It's, without a doubt, the most important question you'll ever be faced with. One that all of us should be deeply concerned with. There are sobering ramifications. Because how we answer that question will profoundly affect every single thing we do in this life. Beyond that, it affects where and how each of us will spend eternity. That's a very sobering thought! Since God has been misrepresented by some of those who should know Him best, and because of untold millions who only know Him based on what someone else has said about Him, the question of, Who God Is, must undoubtedly be put on the list of *The Best Kept Secrets In The Kingdom*.

You're obviously wondering if this is the most important question we'll ever be faced with why in the world would I arrange it at the end of this book. Great question. It's not an oversight on my part. Much to the contrary, it is a calculated decision to put it here. In the few years leading up to 1984, I had lost my way. My marriage was over, and there was no hope for it to recover. My wife and two little boys were gone. I was alone on a ranch 30 miles from town. It was the darkest time of my life. I had a great family and a lot of good friends, but I was in a place where no one could help me. At least that's what I thought. On November 17, 1984, I sat on the edge of my bed, crying my eyes out with no one to turn to. In desperation, I called out to God with this verbatim plea: "God, if You're out there, you gotta help me." I had no reason to believe He would help me. I'd obviously done nothing for Him. Being totally honest with myself, I'd say He had no good reason to answer my hopeless, desperate, and outrageous plea, either. But He did!

I knew nothing about God. I knew nothing about trusting Him. I knew nothing about walking by faith. I didn't even know that to have a relationship with God was anything you could or should do! I was in a suspended state of desperation. What I thought was the worst part of my life has turned out to be the very best. It was there that night, broken and defeated with no hope that I met the Father.

That started an incredible journey, one that continues today, of learning to understand Who God is. I didn't have the terminology of God as a Father in 1984. It came along years later. Over time, God began to open my eyes to Who He really is.

Andy R. Taylor
He is a Father!

The question, "Who Is God?" cannot adequately be answered in one chapter of a book like this one. In fact, that question can't be totally answered in a thousand books with a thousand pages each. I am now in the process of writing a book that will be the defining work of my life. It's a book about The Father. Please pray for me as I write it. Until it's available, run to Him! He's better than we thought! He loves you more than you can imagine!

Trinity Fellowship Vision

Helping One Another Engage In An Intimate Relationship
With The Father Building A Biblical Model of "Family"
Through Personal Relationships

1. RE-CENTERING CENTER
- Integrate Our Culture With the Reality of Jesus and the Father in a Non-Invasive Way
- Creating an Atmosphere for the Supernatural Work of the Holy Spirit
- "Equipping the Saints for the Work of the Ministry"
- Equipping each family member to be a functional contributor in the Body of Christ
- Helping Each Family Member Mature and Fulfill Their Personal Call
- A Ministry School With a 'Hands On' Format
- Training and Sending Out Leaders Locally, Regionally, Nationally and Internationally
- Engaging in an Aggressive Ministry to the Poor
- Outreach Projects/Camps to Assimilate God's Kingdom into Our Culture

2. THE "JUNIPER TREE"
- A Ministry of Restoration and Encouragement to Those in Ministry Who Have Been Wounded or Discouraged in the Process of Their Ministry
- A Focus on Healing Hurts and Wounds Through Love, Encouragement and Scriptural Counseling
- A Resolve to See Individuals/Ministries Restored and Functioning Again in Their Call

Taking care of people = Job #1

Meeting the natural and spiritual needs of individuals and families that God has entrusted to us will always be out #1 priority. This includes all aspects of 'taking care of people'! Nothing is more important.

OUTREACH

3. MINISTRY OVERSIGHT
- Provide Accountability, Adjustment and Training Support For Traveling Ministries
- Provide a Place for Rest, Refocus, Relaxation, Training and Encouragement

4. MINISTRY TEAMS/WORSHIP TEAMS
- Organize, Train and Send Out Ministry Teams
- Assist Struggling Churches By a Team Ministry Concept
- Send Worship Teams to Assist Churches

5. CHURCH PLANTING
- Plant, Support and Staff Churches
- Provide People/Resources to Help the New Church Flourish
- Train and Ordain Leadership in Each Church
- Maintain an Ongoing Supportive Relationship With Each Church

6. CHURCH FATHERING
- Establish the Biblical Pattern for Church Government
- Provide Oversight, Accountability, Adjustment and Support for Existing Churches
- Foster Authentic Relationships Within Churches/Church Leadership
- Restore/Repair Relationships Within the Church

"BUILDING WITH PURPOSE FOR THE NEXT GENERATION"

About the Author

Andy Taylor is the founder and leader of Trinity Fellowship in Sayre, Oklahoma. His ministry has been focused in helping people of all ages learn to relate to God as Father, as well as helping them find their individual gifts enabling them to be functional contributors to the Body of Christ. He's involved in giving apostolic oversight to a growing number of churches and ministries across the Western United States, Canada and Mexico. Andy's profound ability to make complex scriptural issues simple and practical is his key to "equipping the saints for the work of the ministry", and to have a living and powerful Kingdom church that impacts the community, the region, and the nations. A former professional bull rider, Andy was inducted into the Texas Rodeo Cowboy Hall of Fame in 2008. Andy and his wife Julie have been married for 43 years and are proud parents of five grown children and ten grandchildren.

Follow Andy on Twitter - @AndyrtaylorCom

Read his blog: "The Way I See It" - www.andyrtaylor.com

Trinity Fellowship, Sayre, OK - www.justasyouare.com

Email: ATRYB124@gmail.com

To schedule a *The Best Kept Secrets In The Kingdom* Conference call Trinity Fellowship @ 580.928.2345.